FAIR VALUE AND PENSION FUND MANAGEMENT

FAIR VALUE AND PENSION FUND MANAGEMENT

Edited by

NIELS KORTLEVE
PGGM, Kroostweg-Noord 149
PO Box 117, Zeist 3700 AC, The Netherlands

THEO NIJMAN
Tilburg University (and Netspar)
PO Box 90153, Tilburg 5000 LE, The Netherlands

EDUARD PONDS
ABP Pension Fund (and Netspar), PO BOX 75753
WTC Schipol Airport, Schipol 1118 ZX, The Netherlands

ELSEVIER

Amsterdam • Boston • Heidelberg • London • New York • Oxford
Paris • San Diego • San Francisco • Singapore • Sydney • Tokyo

ELSEVIER
The Boulevard, Langford Lane, Kidlington, Oxford OX5 1GB, UK
Radarweg 29, PO Box 211, 1000 AE Amsterdam, The Netherlands

First edition 2006

Notice
No responsibility is assumed by the publisher for any injury and/or damage to persons
or property as a matter of products liability, negligence or otherwise, or from any use or
operation of any methods, products, instructions or ideas contained in the material herein.
Because of rapid advances in the medical sciences, in particular, independent
verification of diagnoses and drug dosages should be made

British Library Cataloguing in Publication Data
A catalogue record for this book is available from the British Library

ISBN-13: 978-0-444-52245-0
ISBN-10: 0-444-52245-X

For information on all Elsevier publications
visit our website at books.elsevier.com

Printed and bound in The Netherlands

06 07 08 09 10   10 9 8 7 6 5 4 3 2 1

Working together to grow
libraries in developing countries

www.elsevier.com | www.bookaid.org | www.sabre.org

ELSEVIER   BOOK AID
International   Sabre Foundation

Foreword

Economists have long advocated the principle of 'mark-to-market' in financial reporting. Indeed, in introductory courses in economics students are routinely taught that the cost of acquiring an asset – its historical cost – becomes a progressively inferior indicator of its 'opportunity cost' with the passage of time. Opportunity cost is the relevant measure for decisions about resource allocation, and opportunity cost is best represented by an accurate estimate of the asset's *current* market price. Fair value accounting is a broad-based movement among scholars, regulators and managers to align the practice of financial reporting with this basic principle of economics.

The papers collected in this volume are about the application of fair value principles to accounting for pensions and its consequences for pension policy. By comparison with valuing the vast bulk of corporate assets and liabilities, the market values of pension plan assets and liabilities can be estimated relatively accurately. Nevertheless, pension accounting has been, and largely still is, one of the most arcane and opaque areas of financial reporting because fair value principles are not applied. Numerous studies have documented the distorting effects that those accounting practices have had on corporate pension funding and asset allocation decisions. I applaud the authors and editors of this book for their rigorous analysis of this subject and for producing an excellent set of papers that can help guide pension accounting reform.

According to new rules adopted by the International Accounting Standards Board, certain fair value principles will have to be applied starting in the year 2006. The publication of this book now is thus just-in-time. It offers great value to pension professionals, pension fund trustees, regulators and indeed anyone with a serious interest in pension policy.

Robert C. Merton[1]

[1]Robert C. Merton is John and Natty McArthur University Professor at the Harvard Business School. He received the Alfred Nobel Memorial Prize in the Economic Sciences in 1997.

Contents

PART I

General

Fair Value and Pension Fund Management
N. Kortleve, T. Nijman and E. Ponds (Editors)
© 2006 Elsevier B.V.

CHAPTER 1

Introduction to 'Fair Value and Pension Fund Management'

Niels Kortleve (PGGM), Theo Nijman (Tilburg University and Netspar) and
Eduard Ponds (ABP and Netspar)

1.1. The fair value method versus the traditional actuarial approach

Risk management by pension funds recently has gone through a process of fundamental change with the substitution of the fair valuation framework for the traditional actuarial approach. This far-reaching change is driven in particular by the move to fair value principles in both accounting standards as well as in supervision (in particular in Europe like UK, the Netherlands and Scandinavia). The actuarial approach is typically grounded on rules of thumb with respect to valuation and accounting issues. The valuation of indexed pension liabilities usually is based on a fixed discount rate that is related to assumed rate of return on assets. The main goal of the actuarial approach has been to arrive at stability in the contribution rate and the funding ratio over time. Risk may be recognized by the actuarial approach, however prudence usually is taken into account by a subjective downward adjustment of the discount rate. The actuarial approach leads to a self-constructed representation of the solvency position of the pension fund without any link to financial markets.

The actuarial approach recently has been heavily criticized[1] (e.g. Exley *et al.*, 1997; Chapman *et al.*, 2001; Bader and Gold, 2002). The approach contrasts sharply with the worldwide trend in accounting standards and supervision towards more transparency through market-based reporting

---

[1] Also the role of the actuarial function in the process of funding and disclosure is being discussed in a rather fundamental way and this will lead without any doubt to changes in the current practice. One may expect that the actuarial function no longer will be exclusively restricted to actuaries but also accessible for professionals with a different but even suitable background, like financial economists and accountants. The actuarial profession will not be discussed in this book.

based on fair value principles. Fair value implies that a pension fund's liability has to be seen as a financial contract. A pension promise is a bond-like asset and has to be valued as a bond. The fair value approach relies on methods of financial theory and techniques prevailing in the financial markets. The main goal is to make an objective analysis of the solvency position of the pension fund and the implied risks in meeting the promised pension benefits. Marking to market will inevitably lead to high volatility in the value of liabilities and assets under management. In particular the liabilities will become much more volatile in the fair value approach compared to the actuarial approach, as the actuarial fixed rate of discount is replaced by the actual yield curve prevailing in the market. However, market valuation of liabilities opens up the possibility of liability-driven investment policies as assets and liabilities are being valued in an equal way. The investment policy in the traditional actuarial approach had by nature no relationship with the pension fund liabilities. This may explain that till recently the investment policy of the pension funds worldwide has been characterized as herding behaviour, by which we mean that pension funds in specific regions roughly hold the same strategic asset mix. Compare Ambachtsheer (2003) for a view on the typical mix for the US, Canada, Australia and European funds. The fair value approach invites pension funds or you may also say force pension funds to relate the mix specifically to their own liabilities.

The scheme below highlights the differences between the two approaches at key aspects.

Aspect	Traditional actuarial approach	Fair value approach
Valuation	Rules of thumb	Market consistent
Risk	Assumed; Smoothing	Actual; Explicit
Aim	Stability in contribution rate and funding ratio over time	Full disclosure financial position; Transparency
Main disadvantage	Self-constructed solvency	Volatility
Investments	Herding; Assets-only	Liability-driven; True ALM
Regulation	Deterministic; Minimum funding ratio	Stochastic analysis; Risk-adjusted minimum funding ratio

1.2. Methods of valuation

Many seemingly different methods have been proposed to value assets and liabilities at market value and all are used in one form or another in the subsequent chapters. Many assets held by pension funds are traded in liquid markets and in these cases the last transaction price is a very good measure of the market value. For some asset classes, including real estate and for the pension fund's liabilities this is typically not the case. Then expert estimates or model-based approaches are typically used. We concentrate on the latter.

If the claim that is to be valued is just a portfolio of existing claims for which market prices are available, the price of the claim will be equal to the price of this portfolio, otherwise arbitrageurs could make an immediate riskless profit. Nominal unconditional pension rights are not different from a bond portfolio if the longevity risk is negligible. Translation of the bond prices to a term structure of interest rates yields that these pension rights can also be simply valued through discounting against the current term structure. If an asset has identical pay-offs to a dynamic portfolio strategy rather than to a static portfolio, the fair value of this asset will be equal to the initial investment to set-up this dynamic strategy. This replication argument underlies the famous Black–Scholes option pricing model as well as all pricing methods in complete markets. Although some methods are written in terms of risk neutral valuation or pricing kernels, either in discrete or in continuous time, all these can be shown to be equivalent to the dynamic replication argument as is explained in numerous text books on derivative pricing.

Valuation in incomplete markets, i.e., valuation of assets that cannot be replicated by trading in other assets, is substantially harder. Introduction of new assets can affect the equilibrium in the economy and the price will usually be derived from arbitrary assumptions on utility functions. Often also direct assumptions on risk premia have been made. Real pension rights cannot be priced using replication arguments if no suitable indexed bonds are traded. If one is willing to assume that inflation risk is not priced, real claims can simply be valued in this incomplete market by discounting against the nominal term structure minus expected inflation.

1.3. Fair valuation at work

The step-over to fair value will imply a lot of changes for the management of a pension fund and for its stakeholders. Below we list a number of issues that will be hit by the introduction of fair value principles (not being meant to be exhaustive).

1. Contribution rate: the new approach enables to determine the true economic costs of newly accruing liabilities due to an additional year

of service. The funding policy may result in an actual contribution rate below the fair value contribution rate, however it is possible then to determine the magnitude of subsidizing the new rights.

2. Labour agreement negotiations: fair value principles shed light on the monetary value of elements of agreements on pension deals, so one may come to a fair-value neutral exchange of labour income today for labour income later as retirement income. Proper valuation makes it possible to arrive at a fair comparison of the costs and the risks of alternatives in pension plan design.

3. Transfers of value: fair valuation models a pension fund as a zero-sum game in terms of economic value; alternatives in pension fund policy strategy produce no economic value, however they may well lead to transfers of value between the stakeholders where the gain for one of the stakeholders is a loss for one or more of the other stakeholders (Kortleve and Ponds, 2006).

4. Corporate finance: the fair value approach implies a full integration of the pension fund balance with the balance sheet of the sponsoring company. The financial position of the pension fund will have a direct impact via the funding residue (surplus or deficit) on the value of the firm for the shareholders. Moreover the riskiness of the pension fund may deviate from the riskiness of the core business of the company and so the explicit recognition of the pension fund being part of the balance sheet of the firm may hit the firm's cost of capital (Lin *et al.*, 2004).

5. Integral risk management: The use of fair value principles makes it possible to analyse the relevant risks within one framework wherein all risks are comparable with each other.

6. Supervisory authority: the fair value approach enables the supervisor to arrive at true assessment of the solvency position of the pension fund, as the pension fund has to report on the true value of assets and liabilities and the impact on the risk position of the pension fund.

1.4. Future developments

One might say that the introduction of fair value principles can be seen as a real revolution for the practice of pension funds. The first victim of this revolution has been the actuarial profession as they had to accept that part of the methods they were used to have been overruled by the methodology of finance and economics. The next victim will be the community of investors, as they have to accept the substitution of liability-driven investment policy for the traditional asset-only orientation with a lot of herding behaviour in it. Then the pension plan design itself may be hit by the move to fair value. Aspects like transparency, accountability and a fair compensation for risk-taking by stakeholders may be in conflict with classical pension plan design solutions. The challenge for the pension fund industry is to find new answers adapted to meet the new challenges posed forward by the introduction of fair value principles.

1.5. Contents of the book

A short description is given for each of the 10 chapters of this book.

Part I: General

1. 'Introduction' to the book by the editors Niels Kortleve (PGGM), Theo Nijman (Tilburg University and Netspar) and Eduard Ponds (ABP and Netspar).
2. 'Pension Funds at Risk' by Casper van Ewijk and Martijn van de Ven (CPB) will shed some light on the current pension fund crisis and how pension funds got there. Their focus is mainly on Dutch pension funds. They close their contribution with a critical evaluation of risk-taking and risk-sharing.
3. 'Building Better Pension Plans on a "Fair Value" foundation' by Keith Ambachtsheer (Rotman, ICPM). Ambachtsheer will discuss how a fair pension deal could be formulated in the new world. He will describe the elements that should be included and the process how to weigh various elements like certainty, price and ambition.

Part II: Technical

4. 'The Fair Value Principle' by Jon Exley, he sets out the basic economic principles behind the fair value method, like replication and the Law of One Price. He also explains that applying fair value method is beneficial to the welfare of the economy. Exley will also pay some attention to the cons of fair value brought up by doubters.
5. 'Techniques for Market-Consistent Valuation of Contingent Claims' by John Hibbert, Steven Morrison and Craig Turnbull (Barrie & Hibbert).

Hibbert *et al.* will describe the technique to value conditional cash flows (contingent claims), like conditional indexation. This technique has been used for almost thirty years in the world of option pricing, but now is applied to pensions.

6. 'Valuation and Risk Management of Inflation-Sensitive Pension Rights' by Theo Nijman (Tilburg University) and Ralph Koijen (Tilburg University). Nijman and Koijen will discuss how to calculate the fair valuation of contracts that offer indexation provided the investment returns are adequate. Option pricing is used to discuss valuation of pension liabilities that are nowadays quite common in the Netherlands and cannot be valued using standard discounting methods.

7. 'Fair Value of Pension Fund Liabilities and Consequences for Strategic Asset Allocation' by Anthony Foley (D.E. Shaw Investment Management, L.L.C.), Andrei Serjantov and Ralph Smith (Advanced Research Center, State Street Global Advisors). This chapter discusses the use of the Merton intertemporal utility-maximization framework in the context of 'fair' valuation of liabilities. In particular, Foley *et al.* introduce and review the model, and discuss its limitations together with the choices of parameters. Finally, they provide a simple 'real world' case study, which contrasts the practice of fair valuation of liabilities with the current approach.

Part III: Application

8. 'Fair Value Accounting and Pension Benefit Guarantees' by Zvi Bodie (Boston University School of Management). Bodie puts forward that fair value accounting is critical for government supervision aimed at protecting pension plan beneficiaries. The focus is on the role of the Pension Benefit Guaranty Corporation (PBGC) in the United States, however main conclusions from the PBGC may also be applied to other countries with a different supervisory system, like the Netherlands.

9. 'Value and Risk Sharing in Defined Benefit Pension Plans' by Andrew Smith (Deloitte). Smith will show how one can use fair value to calculate the stakes of the stakeholders. By looking at the stakes and comparing pension deals, one can optimize the pension deal to achieve the desired targets.

10. 'Pension Deals and Value-Based ALM' by Niels Kortleve (PGGM) and Eduard Ponds (ABP and Netspar). Kortleve and Ponds claim fair value

principles will lead inevitably to value-based ALM. They analyse an industry pension fund with a standard wage-indexed defined benefit scheme with conditional indexation. Within this framework, they show stepping over from *classical ALM* to *value-based ALM* will contribute to the establishment of better and more sustainable pension deals.

References

Ambachtsheer, K. (2003), "An anatomy of pension fund behaviour (1993–2002): What can we learn?" (part I and part II), *The Ambachtsheer Letter*, Letter #214 and Letter #215, November 2003 and December 2003.

Bader, L.N. and J. Gold (2002), "Reinventing pension actuarial science", Available at http://users.erols.com/jeremygold/papers.html

Chapman, R.J., T.J. Gordon and C.A. Speed (2001), "Pensions, funding and risk", *British Actuarial Journal*, Vol. 7, No. 4, pp. 605–663.

Exley, J., S.J.B. Mehta and A.D. Smith (1997), "The financial theory of defined benefit schemes", *British Actuarial Journal*, Vol. 3, No. 4, p. 938.

Kortleve, C.E. and E.H.M. Ponds (2006), "Pension Deals and Value-based ALM", *this volume*.

Lin, L., R. Merton and Z. Bodie (2004), *"Do a Firm's Equity Returns Reflect the Risk of its Pension Plans?"*, Working paper #10650, NBER.

Fair Value and Pension Fund Management
N. Kortleve, T. Nijman and E. Ponds (Editors)
© 2006 Elsevier B.V.

CHAPTER 2

Pension Funds at Risk

Casper van Ewijk and Martijn van de Ven (CPB)

Keywords: retirement saving, risk sharing, transparency, macroeconomic shocks

JEL codes: E44, G23

2.1. Introduction[1]

The Dutch pension system has been much acclaimed as a sound basis for accommodating an ageing population. As supplement to the public pension, substantial funds have been accumulated in the second pillar funds, i.e., the industry and company pension funds. These funds, whose amount comfortably exceeds the country's national debt, play an important role in the economy. The pension system not only offers good income prospects for present and future generations, it also takes care of intergenerational risk sharing, since both windfalls and setbacks can be shared with younger, working generations. The solidarity among generations contributes to making the economy more resilient to shocks.

In recent times, however, it seems that pension funds in the Netherlands are above all a source of economic distortion. Owing to the huge losses on investment portfolios, the conventional funding ratio[2] of pension funds has on average declined from about 150% in 1999 to a minimum of 109% in 2002. Since then it has recovered to reach approximately 120% in 2004. However, most pension funds aim at wage or price indexed retirement benefits. The fair value funding ratio for these indexed liabilities is much lower.

---

[1]This article is an updated and partly rewritten version of van Ewijk and van de Ven (2003).
[2]The conventional funding ratio is based on a 4% discount rate.

By the end of 2002, it measured approximately 80%, preliminary estimates for 2004 indicate a fair value funding ratio of 95%.

Making good the losses required drastic adjustments to pension contribution rates or indexation. In the period to 2007, pension contribution rates are expected to rise by more than 4% points on average. Pension funds are also reducing their indexing of pension rights to prices and wages. This puts further pressure on an already unsettled economy. For the years 2000–2006, approximately 90 000 people lose their jobs due to the higher pension contributions. This illustrates the continued effect of pension fund shocks on the Dutch economy.

What is causing these shocks? Are there reasons to be concerned about the ability of the working population to cope with these risks, now and in the future? What are the implications for the supervision of pension funds? Should it take the system risks of pension funds more into account?

2.2. Growing pension assets

The assets covering collective pension schemes constitute an ever-larger part of the total assets in the Netherlands. In 2003, the accumulated assets at pension funds amounted to 105% of GDP. Including the assets accumulated at life insurance companies for collective pension schemes, this figure becomes approximately 130% of GDP. Figure 2.1 gives an overview of the development of assets accumulated in pension funds since 1990.

Pension fund assets have grown from approximately 70% of GDP in 1991 to 120% of GDP in 1999, at the top of the stock market boom. Since then they have declined to somewhat below 100% of GDP in 2002. By the end of 2003, due to higher contributions and cuts in indexation, pension fund assets had grown to 105% of GDP.

Several factors account for the growth of pension fund assets over the past decades. First, more employees gained access to a collective pension scheme. Also, the maturation of pension funds leads to a growth in assets. Lastly, in recent years the pay-as-you-go early retirement schemes have been gradually replaced by funded pre-pension schemes. Also developments in the stock market had significant effects on the value of pension fund assets, notably the boom in the second half of the 1990s that was followed by the decline in stock market prices at the start of the new millennium.

The ratio between pension fund assets and GDP will further increase in the decades ahead. Table 2.1 gives an estimate of the growth in the assets

Figure 2.1. Pension funds' assets 1991–2003[3]

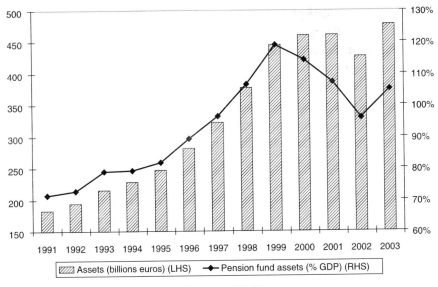

Source: DNB

Table 2.1. Changes in the assets of pension funds 2001–2060

	2001	2020	2040	2060
Pension fund assets (% GDP)	132	172	195	181

Source: van Ewijk *et al.* (2000)

of pension funds. Up to 2040, the assets of pension funds are expected to
increase to nearly twice the GDP. This rise is related to the further maturation
of pension funds on the one hand, and to the increase in the average age of
pension plan members due to an ageing population on the other.

2.3. Larger equity portfolios

Significant shifts are also occurring within the portfolios of pension funds.
In the past ten years, pension funds increased investments in equity from

---

[3]Not included are the assets of collective life insurance arrangements.

Figure 2.2. Pension funds' investment portfolio mix, 1990–2002

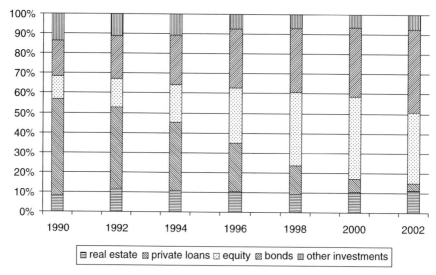

real estate private loans equity bonds other investments

Source: DNB

about 10% of their investments in 1990 to almost 40% in 2002. Figure 2.2 shows the changes in the average investment portfolio of pension funds. The expansion in equity ownership has been mostly at the expense of private loans.

2.4. Declining returns

The larger share of risk-bearing investments initially resulted in pension funds benefiting significantly from the rise in share prices. By the same token, the changed portfolios have made pension funds equally sensitive to declining share prices, as became evident in recent years.

Figure 2.3 shows the changes in assets and percentage returns as from 1991. The left axis shows the assets of the company, industry and occupational pension funds in billions of euro. The right axis shows the return.

It is clearly visible that in the latter half of the 1990s, returns were high and that the assets of pension funds increased substantially in this period. The new millennium had a considerably worse start, with negative returns even causing the assets of pension funds to shrink in 2001 and 2002. In 2003 returns were close to 10%. The first reports in 2004 indicate similar returns as in 2003.

Figure 2.3. *Assets (in billions of euro) and return (in percent) of pension funds*

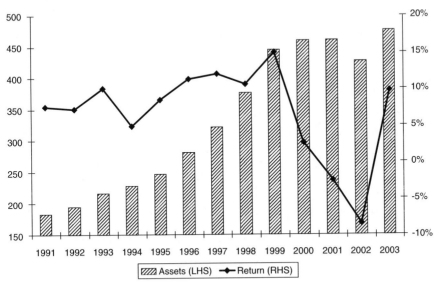

Source: DNB; own computations

2.5. Lower funding ratios

The low returns led to a sharp fall in the funding ratio, an indicator of the extent to which the liabilities of pension funds are covered by their assets.

Figure 2.4 shows the changes in the funding ratio. Both the conventional 4% funding ratio as a fair value funding ratio is shown (see box 'market valuation'). First examine the conventional 4% funding ratio. In the latter half of the 1990s, this funding ratio went up significantly. The low returns since 2000 led to a fall in the funding ratio from 150% in 1999 to 109% at the start of 2003. Preliminary calculations indicate that by the end of 2004 it reached 120%.

A more dramatic picture emerges if we look at fair value funding ratios.[4] Both the funding ratio of the nominal as of the indexed liabilities[5] is shown. Both graphs follow a much more volatile path over time. Clearly, due to

---

[4]This calculation was done by the supervisor, the Dutch central bank DNB. It is an indicative calculation based on data of individual pension funds. However, until recently, pension funds had some degree of freedom in reporting the value of their assets and liabilities.

[5]i.e., indexation to prices.

Figure 2.4.   Changes in the funding ratio of pension funds 1988–2004

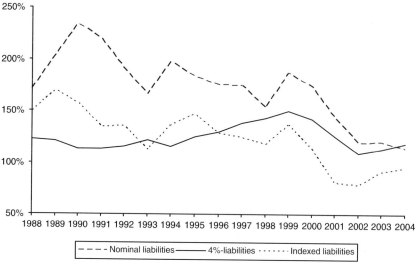

Source: DNB

the adverse stock market developments, these funding ratios declined as well from 1999 onwards. However, the decline in the fair value funding ratios started much earlier. The decline prior to 1999 coincides with the decline in interest rates as can be seen from Figure 2.5, which shows the development of the funding ratio of the nominal liabilities and of the nominal interest rate.

Market valuation

According to the arbitrage principle, the value of a pension liability can be derived from the market value of financial assets with a similar risk and duration. Hence, the value of a nominal pension liability can be derived from the value of a bond with identical cash flows. In other words, the value can be calculated by discounting the nominal pension benefit with the interest rate for nominal bonds. In a similar way, the value of other obligations can be calculated by discounting the cash flows with the appropriate discount rate. For indexed linked pension obligations, the appropriate discount rate can be derived from indexed linked bonds. Unfortunately there are no indexed linked bonds available for the Netherlands. Data on indexed linked bonds in e.g. the UK and France can be used to estimate the Dutch real interest rate.

Pension schemes where benefits are linked to wages are more difficult to value since the level of the pension benefit depends on the uncertain wage development. Because there are no assets with similar characteristics, we have to use the existing theories on pricing of risk on capital markets. The basic ideas can be found in the Capital Asset Pricing Model (CAPM): the value of an uncertain cash flow *P* can be calculated by discounting the expected cash flow by the appropriated discount rate:

$$\text{Value} = E(P)/(1 + d)$$

where $E(P)$ is the expected value of an uncertain cash flow *P* and *d* is the appropriate discount rate. The discount rate can be calculated as the sum of the risk free rate (*r*) and a risk premium (*z*):

$$d = r + z$$

According to the CAPM, the risk premium follows from the covariance between the return and the market return or macroeconomic variables like GDP or consumption. The price of risk depends on the degree of risk aversion: a certain cash flow is preferred over an uncertain cash flow. An application of the CAPM for estimation of risk premiums is for example Borensztein and Mauro (2002, 2004). They use the CAPM to derive premiums for GDP indexed bonds. They find fairly low values for the risk premium, below 1%.

Figure 2.5.   The nominal funding ratio and the nominal interest rate

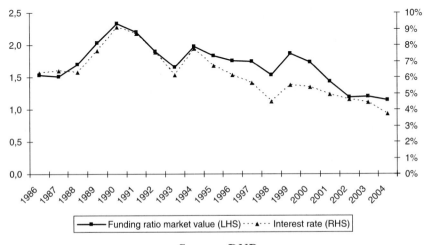

Source: DNB

The difference between the traditional 4% funding ratio and the fair value funding ratios stresses the importance of the fair value approach. The development in assets and liabilities due to, among others, the decline in interest rates remained to a large extent invisible in the traditional 4% funding ratio. So, while in reality the financial position already eroded since the beginning of the 1990s, the general sentiment – misguided by the traditional accounting methods – was one of great optimism about alleged excess reserves, leading to cuts in contribution rates and even premium holidays and to capital transfers to sponsoring companies.

2.6. High level of ambition

The huge capital resources accumulated by pension funds in connection with large investments in equity are responsible for the significant impact of capital losses of pension funds on the Dutch economy. These capital resources of second pillar pension funds are the result of large memberships and – certainly in comparison with other countries – the high level of pensions to which they aspire (cf. Whitehouse, 2002). Virtually all employees are required to join a pension fund. In 1996, 91% of employees between the ages of 25 and 65 years had a supplementary pension provision (SZW/SER, 1996).[6] The origin of the Dutch pension system has strong corporatist characteristics. Pension funds are organised on the basis of industry or business sectors; the amount and nature of pensions are determined by employers and employees. Against this background, a large variety of pension funds and schemes sprang up. Compulsory membership effectively prevents any competition between pension funds.

By far the most second pillar pensions in the Netherlands are defined benefit schemes (see box 'From final pay to average pay'). Most pension funds aim to provide inflation proof pensions, with benefits coupled to wage increases. Benefits usually accrue gradually by means of a fixed percentage of salary (on top of a franchise) per year of service.

The sector-based nature of the Dutch pension system restricts the extent of inter-generational risk sharing. Unlike taxation, where continuity in the tax base is assured, the continuity of pension funds may be jeopardised.

---

[6]The most recent survey dates from 2002 but did not provide comparable data. It was concluded that participation of pension schemes had grown since 1996 (SER, 2002).

From final pay to average pay

Final pay defined benefit schemes used to dominate the Dutch pension landscape. In recent years there has been a gradual shift towards average pay schemes. This table shows the partition of the various types of pension schemes.

Pension funds according to type of pension scheme (primo, 2004)

	Number of funds (% of the total)	Number of active members	Balance sheet total
Defined benefit			
Final pay	46,2	12,5	14,4
Average pay	25,6	74,2	69,9
Other	18,1	10,0	15,0
Defined contribution	8,4	3,2	0,7
Other	1,7	0,1	0,0
Total	100,0	100,0	100,0

Source: DNB, Pension Monitor 2004.

Between 1998 and 2004 the number of active members participating in a final pay schemes has declined with 54,3% point, whereas participation in average pay schemes has grown with 49,5% point. The rest has switched to DC-schemes. As of January 1, 2004 the two largest pension funds in the Netherlands, the civil servant pension fund ABP and the health care and social work sector fund PGGM, have switched from a final pay scheme to an average pay scheme. Because of this, average pay schemes have become the most common type of pension scheme.

Businesses and sectors can contract and even disappear, and employees, too, can try to shirk membership of a given sector's pension fund. This restricts the extent to which pension funds are able to absorb shocks by adjusting the contributions of the active members. Well known are the problems facing pension funds with strongly ageing memberships, and the issue of collapsing sponsors, a danger that mostly faces pension funds whose membership is restricted to a few or a single business.

This is why the rules of most defined benefit schemes include severely restrictive clauses. As a rule, index linking to prices (or wages) has been made subject to the financial position of the fund. Disappointing investment results as well as demographic risks (longevity) can therefore be passed on in part to the pensioners themselves.

The new Financial Assessment Framework (nFTK)

As from January 2007, the new framework of financial assessment of pension funds (nFTK) will come into effect. The main ingredients are:

- Assets and liabilities should be reported at market value;
- Liabilities are distinguished into 'hard' and 'soft' liabilities. Liabilities are hard when they do not depend on a future decision of the pension fund. Soft liabilities, most often the wage or price indexation, require a decision of the pension fund;
- The assets should be sufficient to maintain a funding ratio of at least 105% of the hard liabilities with a probability of 97,5% over a period of one year. This implies that a pension fund with a portfolio of 50% equity and 50% bonds should have a funding ratio of approximately 130% of the hard liabilities.
- Funding ratio's have to be restored within 15 years when the funding ratio is below the required level (but still above 105%). If the funding ratio declines to below 105%, pension funds must in principle restore a funding ratio of at least 105% within one year (apart from exceptional situations).

The switch from an artificial 4% discount rate to market valuation is an important aspect of the nFTK. However, some elements are clear compromises between the different stakeholders. Pension fund do not have to fully fund their indexed liabilities as long as they include some small print in the contract requiring a decision by the board of directors. Furthermore, pension funds with clear explicit indexation rules may even be punished for their transparency if the supervisor regards these rules as hard liabilities.

There is also a focus on nominal guarantees whereas most participants most likely prefer real guarantees since these enable maintaining the standard of living to a certain degree after retirement. The nominal focus may also lead to underfunding of the expected pensions. Furthermore, the nFTK fails to encourage matching between investments and expected, indexed, liabilities.

2.7. Growing risks

Several trends could increase the risks borne by pensioners and those saving for a pension, and affect the basis for absorbing inter-generational risk sharing. These include an ageing population, individualisation and the increasing international mobility of labour. An ageing population means that the ratio of pensioners to those holding down jobs increases, and that the basis for inter-generational risk sharing decreases. This is due to the leverage with which shocks in the pension fund assets are translated into contribution adjustments. The higher the pension assets and liabilities in relation to the

Figure 2.6.   Shrinking contribution base for shocks

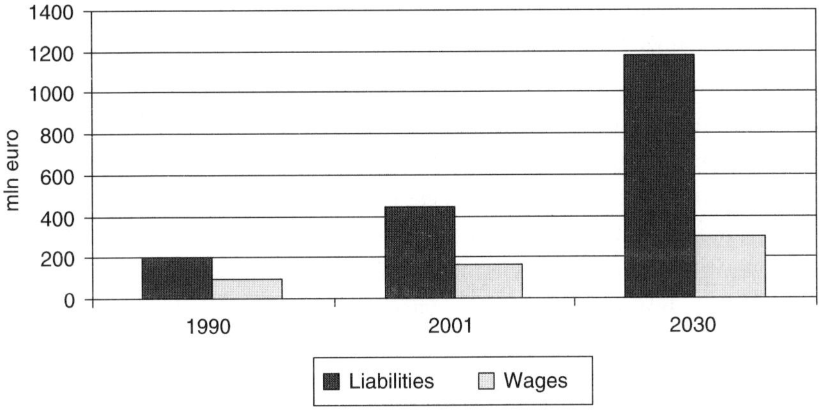

Source: van Ewijk et al. (2000)

number of people in employment, the smaller the pension contribution base becomes. Shocks in investment returns or in pension liabilities will then have to be absorbed by fewer people, so that the leverage with which these shocks affect individual contributions becomes greater. As illustrated in Figure 2.6, relative to the total gross wages, the liabilities of pension funds are set to rise significantly between now and 2030.

The ratio between pension liabilities and total wages goes up from approximately 2,5 now to 4,5 in 2030. As a consequence of this, a negative shock of 10% in pension assets to be made good over ten years in the form of contributions, would result, in 2001, in an average contribution adjustment of 2½% points, whereas in 2030 – because of the smaller contribution base – a contribution adjustment of 4½% points would be required. This is almost twice as much.

The greater volatility of contributions increases the risks for future generations. The question is whether future generations will always be able and willing to absorb the shocks. This question is more important, since new members may be expected in the future to adopt an increasingly critical attitude. In addition, the growing international mobility of labour is providing more and more opportunities for avoiding the burden of contributions. Suppose that, unlike in other sectors or abroad, the contributions to a fund with an ageing membership have to be substantially increased because of disappointing investment results. Compared to a job elsewhere, new members joining such a pension fund would face a capital loss.

2.8. The macroeconomic effects of the current pension shock

Between 1999 and 2006, pension contribution rates are growing from 9,0% of total wages to 14,4%. The fact that contribution rates were below cost level in the second half of the 1990s explains a part of the rise. However, to restore funding ratios, contribution rates had to increase further. The higher contributions not only affect the purchasing power of people in employment, they also affect the labour market (via the wedge) and public sector finances (through the deductibility of contributions). Due to this rise in contribution rates unemployment rises by approximately 90 000 people.

Table 2.2 shows the effects on various macroeconomic variables of the rising pension contribution rates.

In the short term, higher contribution rates imply higher labour costs and, because of lower net wages, lower consumption. This leads to more unemployment: higher labour costs lead to lower labour demand and lower (real) wages depresses labour supply. In the longer term, higher unemployment depresses wages and, thus, labour costs. Hence, unemployment falls but remains higher than before the rise in contribution rates. Tax revenues fall due to lower wages and consumption. This is only partly compensated for by the linking of public sector wages and benefits to lower contractual wages in the market sector. All in all the financing deficit of the government increases.

Although pension funds have several instruments at their disposal to deal with shocks on their assets and liabilities, it was common until recently to counterbalance shocks by adjusting contribution rates. As illustrated above,

Table 2.2.   Effects of the increase in pension contributions in 2000–2006[a]

		2003	2006	2010
		Cumulative Changes		
Contribution rates (% wage sum)	D	4,9	5,4	5,4
Contractual wages market sector	%	−0,2	−3,6	−6,7
Consumer price index	%	1,3	0,7	−1,0
GDP	%	−0,7	−1,9	−1,7
Consumption	%	−0,6	−3,4	−4,5
Employment (% labour years)	D	−0,8	−1,8	−1,3
General government financial balance (% GDP)	D	−1,1	−2,3	−2,7

[a]D indicates absolute differentials; % indicates a relative change.

this has strong negative macroeconomic consequences. Besides, due to the ageing of the population, the contribution base is shrinking. Because of the shrinking contribution base, many pension funds have switched from final pay to average pay and have scaled down their ambition level.

Table 2.3 illustrates the difference for contribution rates and macro-economic variables like employment, consumption in the current recovery trajectory when pension funds shift fully[7] from a final pay system to an average pay system.[8]

The switch to average pay schemes mitigates the rise of contribution rates. This reflects the greater role of indexation cuts in average pay schemes since the indexation of the accumulated rights of active members is reduced. This is beneficial for employment since indexation cuts are less distorting, because there is no direct link to labour supply. Indexation cuts concern the accumulated rights in the past, which have no linkage to current labour supply. This certainly holds for the current retirees. It partly holds for the current active members of the pension scheme. If they expect indexation cuts in the future, these indexation cuts also affect the rights they are accumulating now.

Table 2.3. Economic effects of the switch from final pay to average pay[a]

		2010	2015	2025
		Cumulative Changes		
Contribution rates (% wage sum)	D	−5,5	−4,4	−2,7
Pension payments (% wage sum)	D	−0,2	−0,8	−2,1
Tax revenue (% GDP)	D	0,8	0,6	0,3
Consumption	%	0,1	0,1	0,1
Employment (% labour years)	%	0,1	0,4	0,3
GDP	%	0,4	0,6	0,5
Public debt (% GDP)	D	−3.1	−7,2	−13,7

[a]5-year moving averages over the past 5 years; D indicates absolute differentials to the baseline scenario; % indicates a relative change.

[7]Note that in reality there has been a partial shift from final pay to average pay schemes (see box 'From final pay to average pay'). Hence, the actual economic effects of the shift will be comparably smaller.

[8]The illustration is taken from Westerhout et al. (2004). The simulations were done using the OLG general equilibrium model GAMMA. The results are therefore not fully comparable with this in Table 2.2 which were generated by the short and medium term model SAFFIER. For a general description of GAMMA, see Draper and Westerhout (2002).

The latter point also has negative effects on labour supply that, however, are not counteracting the positive effects on labour supply of indexation cuts.

The beneficial effects on employment, together with the lower contribution rates and higher consumption imply higher tax revenues for the government and, subsequently, lower debt. The positive effect on GDP reflects the effects on employment, consumption, etc.

2.9. How to deal with risks?

Pension funds can take three different types of measures to avoid the macroeconomic spillovers of risks. Firstly, they can reduce the financial risks by opting for a more conservative investment strategy. Secondly, they can adjust the sharing of risks and allocate more of them to the pensioners. Finally, reducing the level of ambition of second pillar pensions can bring down the weight of the risks as well.

When it comes to investment behaviour, there is a trade-off between microefficiency and macroefficiency. From a microeconomic angle, it may be efficient to have a pension fund bear the risks, so that future generations can share these risks. This is true of both investment risks and demographic risks (particularly the longevity risk). From a macroeconomic angle, however, it is desirable to minimise the distorting effects on the economy. In accordance with the tax smoothing principle, fluctuations in the tax and contribution wedge should be avoided as much as possible. Investments in equity, in particular, are detrimental from a macroeconomic angle because they result in a negative covariance between pension contributions and macroshocks in the economy. This means that on average, pension contributions are high when economic conditions are poor and low when conditions are good. Ideally, it should be exactly the opposite. To this end, pension funds should even hold a short position in equity, since on average the windfalls occur in an economic downturn and the setbacks in an economic upturn. This outcome is in line with a survey into the best portfolio mix for the government. For the US, the conclusion of Henning Bohn (1990) is that the stability of public sector finances (and the tax rate) would benefit from a portfolio with a negative position in equity. In that case, lower 'dividend' payments on the public debt compensate on average lower tax revenues because of adverse economic conditions.

A similar approach could be used to the consolidated portfolio of the government and the pension funds in the Netherlands. After all, we are concerned with the combined tax and contribution wedge. The current mix, with the government nominally indebted and the pension sector largely owning equity, is far from ideal from a macroeconomic standpoint. It would be more natural for pension investments to concentrate on fixed income securities, preferably index-linked loans since they provide protection against the risk of inflation. The risks of index linking to real wages are less distorting (or even welcome), since they produce a positive covariance between pension contributions and macroeconomic shocks. The Dutch government could do its bit here by issuing long term bonds and indexed bonds.

Unfortunately, the trade-off between the microefficiency of risk sharing and the macroefficiency of tax smoothing is unavoidable. Where the optimum lies cannot be determined beforehand. For the time being, it would go a little too far to ban pension funds from investing in equity. Having said that, the foregoing is a clear warning signal to pension funds that their strategy should not be too risky.

2.10. Towards a new pension deal

Recent developments in stock markets have made painfully clear the importance of the macroeconomic spillovers of funded second pillar pensions in the Netherlands. The needed increase in pension contributions not only pushes up unemployment, it puts pressure on the government's budget as well. The current shock in the pension system begs the question of how it should deal with the increasing risks.

Apart from greater prudence in investments, modification of the pension deal seems unavoidable as well. The pension system contributes to welfare through the intergenerational sharing of risks. This is not a licence to pass on risks unrestricted to younger generations, however. The support base of young generations is limited and is set to diminish further in the future. Many proposals to solve the 'mid-life' crisis of pension funds are aimed at laying the pension deal on the table to be able to pass on more risks to the pension beneficiaries. Consideration is also being given to the level of pension benefits that funds aspire to. Recently, the two biggest pension funds in the Netherlands, the civil servants' fund ABP and the health care sector fund PGGM, have switched from a final pay system to an average pay system. Index linking to prices and wages is no longer taken as a matter of course either. Some even advocate a complete switch to a (collective) defined contribution system. In that case shocks are accommodated immediately through adjustments of the entitlements.

This gives rise to more fundamental questions. If more risks are passed on to the pensioners, what is then the dividing line with the individual third pillar? Is the value added of the second pillar not found above all in intergenerational risk sharing? When guarantees expire and security diminishes, the value aspect of this insurance depreciates. The question then is whether the choice between return and risk should not be left to the members themselves by releasing part of the pensions to the third pillar.

Lastly, owing to the strongly implicit character of the pension deal, the credibility and transparency of decisions is a primary requirement. In this respect, it is cause for concern that there is the danger of a discrepancy emerging between the perception the public at large has of pensions ('certain and inflation-proof'), and the reality of high-risk pensions. More clarity is urgently required on the sharing of risks among the various stakeholders (including future generations). Who is to absorb the shocks? How certain are the pensions and what minimum guarantees are being offered? Not even the Netherlands, which in an international context seemed for so long to be a safe haven in the field of pensions, will be unable to avoid a broad social debate on this topic. A switch from arbitrary valuation methods to fair value methods reflecting the true market value of pension promises is an important and necessary step for a fruitful discussion on risks and risk sharing.

Literature

Bohn, H. (1990), "Tax smoothing with financial instruments", *The American Economic Review*, 80-5, pp. 1217–1230.

Borensztein, E. and P. Mauro (2002), Reviving the Case for GDP-indexed Bonds, IMF Policy Discussion Paper 02/10.

Borensztein, E. and P. Mauro (2004), "The case for GDP-indexed bonds", *Economic Policy*, April 2004, pp. 165–216.

Draper, N. and E. Westerhout (2002), Ageing, sustainability and the interest rate: the GAMMA model, CPB report 2002/4, pp. 38–41.

Ewijk, C. van (2003), Nieuw pensioenakkoord nodig, ESB, 21 February 2003 (in Dutch).

Ewijk, C. van and M. van de Ven (2002), Pensioenvermogen Vanuit Macro-economisch Perspectief, Preadviezen van de Koninklijke Vereniging voor de Staathuishoudkunde (KVS), Amsterdam (in Dutch).

Ewijk, C. van and M. van de Ven (2003), Pension funds at risk, CPB report 2003/1, pp. 22–27.

Ewijk, C. van, B. Kuipers, H. ter Rele, M. van de Ven and E. Westerhout (2000), Ageing in the Netherlands, CPB/Sdu, The Hague.

SER (The Social and Economic Council of the Netherlands) (2002), rapport Witte vlekken op pensioengebied, quick scan 2001 (in Dutch).

SZW (The Ministry of Social Affairs and Employment)/SER (The Social and Economic Council of the Netherlands) (1996), Witte vlekken op pensioengebied. VUGA The Hague (in Dutch).

Westerhout, E., M. van de Ven, C. van Ewijk and N. Draper (2004), Naar een schokbestendig pensioenstelsel; Verkenning van enkele beleidsopties op pensioengebied, CPB Document 67 (in Dutch).

Whitehouse, E. (2002), Pension Systems in 15 Countries Compared: The Value of Entitlements, Centre for Pensions and Superannuation Discussion Paper 02/04.

Fair Value and Pension Fund Management
N. Kortleve, T. Nijman and E. Ponds (Editors)

CHAPTER 3

Building Better Pension Plans on a 'Fair Value' Foundation

Keith Ambachtsheer[a] (Rotman, ICPM)

Abstract

*We are struck by the continued willingness of people to assume that tra-
ditional DB and DC plans are the only possible answers to the pension
delivery question, and that our only challenge is to figure out which of these
two pension plan options is 'better'. What if we started with the ultimate
pension questions behind the answers? Would those questions logically lead
to DB or DC plans as they currently operate around the world as the only
possible answers? The message of this chapter is 'we think not'.*

*The chapter leads off by first identifying the ultimate pension questions
behind the traditional answers. The best answer to the first of such questions in turn leads to another question and so on. Eventually, this 'answer
and question' process leads to some powerful benchmarks against which to
evaluate the effectiveness of traditional DB and DC plans. The bad news is
that neither of the traditional pension plan formulas score particularly well
on the resulting pension delivery effectiveness scale. The good news is that
our 'answer and question' logic gives clear direction to the search for better
pension models with greater transparency on the extent and the allocation
of risk bearing with a pension plan. It turns out that the 'fair value' concept
offers valuable insight into how this search should be conducted and where
better answers may be found.*

JEL codes: G13, G23, H55 and M41

3.1. Ultimate pension questions and their consequences

So what are the ultimate pension questions and answers with which we
can launch our quest for better answers? We think the first sequence goes

---

[a]Keith Ambachtsheer is Director of The Rotman International Centre for Pension Management at
the University of Toronto, and a strategic advisor to major pension funds around the world.

something like this:

Q: 'What can we do now to ensure the eventual delivery of adequate post-retirement income streams that deal effectively with default risk, re-investment risk, multiple employer risk, inflation risk and longevity risk?'
A: 'By saving the necessary proportion of current income, and investing the proceeds in portable securities that promise default risk-free, life annuities upon retirement with payment streams tied to productivity growth and inflation'.

This answer leads directly to the next ultimate 'Q&A' sequence:

Q: 'Do such securities exist?'
A: 'No'.

So very quickly, our 'Q&A' quest has led to a very important consideration in building better pension delivery models. It is this: there is no market-based security that will deliver a portable, certain, future pension for life, adjusted for productivity growth and inflation. This conclusion leads to an important corollary: either some intermediary underwrites the mismatch risk between the securities that financial markets offer and the ideal pensions people want, or people are going to have to underwrite that mismatch risk themselves.

3.2. Underwriting pension mismatch risk: any volunteers?

So we have logically arrived at our next 'Q&A' sequence:

Q: 'Are there logical third-parties who would willingly underwrite the pension mismatch risk as defined above?'
A: 'Not obviously'.

In national Pillar #1 pay-go pension systems (e.g. the US Social Security system), prior generations decided that pension mismatch risk would be borne by successor generations. Such systems are sustainable as long as contribution rates stay within 'affordable' bounds, and deliver 'reasonable' pensions. Such pay-go systems become unsustainable when the 'affordable contribution rate/reasonable pensions' conditions can no longer be met. In such situations, the intergenerational mismatch risk underwriting process breaks down. As a result, the risks of higher contribution rates and/or lower pensions are crystallized, and pushed back from future to current generations. Specifically, the current generation is forced to either pay more, or receive less. These unpleasant possibilities are finally coming into full view in countries with large Pillar #1 pay-go systems. Change does not come easily in these systems. Current beneficiaries vote, while future contributors do not. Nevertheless, some combination of later retirement dates and contained benefits will eventually be required to keep these systems sustainable.

What about Pillar #2 workplace pension plans? Are there natural pension mismatch risk underwriters here? What about current employers? Maybe, maybe not. On one end of the spectrum, we could visualize broad tax-payer groups having considerable pension mismatch risk underwriting capacity in their role as public sector employers. On the other hand, we could visualize small corporate employers not having any such capacity at all. Of course there is a difference between having pension mismatch risk underwriting capacity and actually putting that capacity 'in play'. Putting it 'in play' implies an employer should ensure that its use of pension risk underwriting capacity is properly valued as a component of total compensation, that this value is understood/appreciated by current employees, and that it is clear how and by whom pension mismatch risk is being underwritten.

In this context, what about future employers (e.g. ultimately the future taxpayers or shareholders), and for that matter, future employee/pension plan members themselves as pension mismatch risk underwriters? These future groups are tempting targets for today's employers and plan members, as these future groups are not at the table today to defend their economic interests. Not surprisingly, 'real world' pension deals often push pension mismatch risk bearing ahead to these future groups. For example, the 2005 Annual Report of the Ontario Teachers' Pension Plan noted that C$20 billion of balance sheet gains over the course of the 1990s were converted into increased benefits and lower contribution rates. The Report also noted that the Plan's funding shortfall at the end of 2004 was also C$20 billion, which will have to be made up by increased contributions in the future.

Fairness and plan sustainability both argue for properly valuing the use of pension risk underwriting capacity, especially if it is on behalf of people not at the table today. In other words, tomorrow's risk bearers should not be put in a position where they are bearing risk in a way where they can only lose, or at best only break even. If they are being put in a position where they can lose, they should be fairly compensated for their risk underwriting role. Further, their risk exposure should be bounded so as not to be so large as to motivate them to break the contract if potential risks turn into reality and become too financially burdensome to bear.

So again, our 'Q&A' quest leads to an important conclusion: the most obvious third-party candidates for bearing pension mismatch risk are future generations of employers and employees. However, if intergenerational risk transfer 'deals' are to be fair and sustainable, they must be transparent, properly valued, symmetrical and bounded.

3.3. Should pension mismatch risk be minimized?

Let us go back for a moment to the 'perfect pension' formula (i.e., a portable, adequate post-retirement income stream with zero default, inflation and longevity risk). We noted that the financial markets do not offer securities that are perfect hedges against such 'perfect pension' promises. This raises yet another ultimate question:

Q: 'What could be done to minimize "perfect pension" mismatch risk?'
A: 'Two steps would go a long way towards achieving a pension risk minimization objective.'

These two steps are:

1. Pool longevity/mortality risk among large groups of participants, making self-insurance a practical alternative, as the longevity/mortality risk characteristics of large participant groups are highly predictable (a caveat here is the observation that actuaries have systematically underestimated longevity 'risk' for decades now, by not factoring increasing life expectancies into their actuarial models).
2. Use long term, default risk-free, inflation-linked financial securities (e.g. inflation-linked bonds issued by the default risk-free entities such as G-7 sovereign issuers) to lay off the default and inflation risk elements of the 'perfect pension' contract.

The problem with this 'solution' is that the cost of delivering the 'perfect pension' works out to 25–30% of pay on a 'fair value' basis. This is too expensive! Thus the next 'Q&A' sequence becomes:

Q: 'What can be done to make the "perfect pension" more affordable?'
A: 'Take investment risk, earn a "risk premium", and use the extra expected return to reduce the expected contribution rate'.

With long investment horizons and the magic of compounding, it is true that 25–30% of pay contribution rates can be magically shrunk to 15% or even less, if a 2–3% excess return over inflation-linked bond returns is in fact earned over the long run.

Now we are getting into familiar territory. By the late 1990s, it had become an article of faith that such excess returns were indeed available to long term investors, and that hence 'perfect pensions at bargain prices' were available to all who subscribed to this long term view. The four year 2000–2003 period has reminded all of us that the long run is made up of a successive series of shorter runs, each of which must be survived in order to get to that nirvana-like 'long run'.

So with this new knowledge painfully acquired over the 2000–2003 period, where do we stand on the pension mismatch risk question now? It seems to us that we have learned that risk minimization is not a strategy that should be automatically dismissed, even if it implies scaling down pension promises to more affordable levels. If, however, decisions are taken to continue to reach for excess returns, surely the experience of the last three years has taught us that such decisions should not be taken casually. Further, we better be sure we understand which parties are going to be underwriting what 'pension deal' risks, so that we can measure the amount of risk being taken, that the risk underwriting function is being properly rewarded, and that the financial consequences of potential risk exposure becoming reality are bounded, and hence sustainable.

3.4. 'Fair Value' and risk disclosure

To fully understand the importance of this risk disclosure requirement, consider the two DB pension plan balance sheet cases depicted in Figure 3.1. The top panel depicts a DB plan balance sheet where there is no asset/liability mismatch risk. The notes below this balance sheet explain why it passes the 'full disclosure' test: there are no undisclosed risks on the balance sheet. Now look at the bottom panel which depicts a DB plan where there is asset/liability mismatch risk. Now the simple disclosure of the market values of the hard asset and liabilities no longer passes the 'full disclosure' test. This is so, even if these assets and liabilities disclosures meet the 'fair value' test. Why? Because, as the notes point out, there is now a web of contingent claims on the balance sheet that should also be disclosed.

Without the disclosure of these contingent claims, and the disclosure of their respective values on the balance sheet valuation date, DB balance sheet stakeholders are left partially in the dark. This is especially the case when the value of the 'Musical Chairs' (i.e., unallocated risks) option is material.

Figure 3.1.   'Fair value' DB pension plan balance sheets including disclosure of contingent claims

Balance Sheet #1: No A/L Mismatch Risk

Hard Assets	Hard Liabilities
Matched Bond Portfolio $100	PV of future pension payments $100

Notes to balance sheet:

- Hard Liabilities are the Present Value (PV) of a payment stream discounted on a market-determined yield curve basis.
- Hard Assets are a portfolio of default risk-free bonds that match the payment obligations, marked to market.
- In the absence of A/L mismatch risk, this DB balance sheet passes the 'full disclosure' test.

Balance Sheet #2: With A/L Mismatch Risk

Hard Assets	Hard Liabilities
Risky Investment Portfolio (e.g. equities) $100	PV of future pension payments $100

Contingent Assets		Contingent Liabilities	
Claim on additional contributions	$a	Claim on additional benefits	$b
Option to reduce benefits	$c	Claim on excess hard assets	$d
'Musical Chairs' option to wait and see what happens and sort things out later	$e	'Musical Chairs' option to wait and see what happens and sort things out later	$f

Notes to balance sheet:

- Hard Liabilities are the PV of a payment stream discounted on a market-determined yield curve basis
- Hard Assets are a portfolio of equities marked to market.
- However, disclosing only the values of 'Hard' assets and liabilities in the presence of balance sheet mismatch risk no longer satisfies any reasonable 'full disclosure' test. Contingent assets and liabilities should also be disclosed.
- Contingent Liabilities are options on potential additional benefits and/or potential excess hard assets.

Figure 3.1.—cont'd

- Contingent Assets are options to reduce potential benefits and/or claims on additional financial resources in case of potential hard asset shortfalls.
- If the 'Musical Chairs' options have a positive value (i.e., $e and $f are positive), the 'pension deal' has not been fully defined, meaning that possible future deficits have not been contractually converted to either additional contributions or reduced benefits.
- If the 'Musical Chairs' option has a zero value, the respective values of the two contingent asset and liability options (i.e., $a, $b, $c, $d) will indicate the degree to which the 'pension deal' is fair, or whether it favours one (or more) stakeholder groups at the expense of another(s). An example of an unfair pension deal would be a case where one stakeholder groups 'owns' all the contingent claims on surplus hard assets i.e., $b+$d), while another stakeholder group is liable for providing all the additional financial resources in the case of potential hard asset shortfalls (i.e., $a+$c).

Its value indicates the size of the 'undefined' part of the defined benefit plan. In other words, it is the 'fair value' estimate of the DB balance sheet not explicitly assigned to any stakeholder group as either a 'contingent obligation to pay more', or a 'contingent obligation to take a lower benefit'. Surely this is material information that should be disclosed to all balance sheet stakeholders. A word of caution to readers: to simplify the balance sheets, we assume 'closed' DB plans. This eliminates the complicating need to deal with future benefit accruals and future 'normal' contributions.

3.5. Four further insights

Figure 3.1 has already demonstrated how the extended balance sheet approach offers powerful insights into DB plan risk bearing. Four further insights are:

- While Balance Sheet #2 provides material additional information when there is DB balance sheet mismatch risk, it still does not provide the total picture. In the limit, each stakeholder 'cohort', and ultimately each individual stakeholder in the DB balance sheet, has her/his own unique claims/obligations to hard and contingent assets and liabilities. This reality lays bare the unavoidable complexity embedded in any DB scheme created by risk sharing. Thus it also highlights a fundamental advantage embedded in pension schemes based on capital accumulation with the ability to convert financial capital into life annuities. In the USA, the TIAA-CREF pension system for university employees is a good example of such a scheme.

- There are two types of 'Options to reduce benefits' in Balance Sheet #2 case. First, there might be an explicit formula to reduce benefits in an ongoing context in certain pre-defined conditions. Second, there is the default context where the benefit reduction occurs because there are insufficient hard assets at the point of bankruptcy of the pension plan sponsor.

- This bankruptcy-driven 'option to reduce benefits' really is a subset of the 'Musical Chairs' option. That is, things are sorted out only if a bankruptcy actually occurs. The existence/non-existence of a pension payment insurance scheme (e.g. the PBGC in the USA) becomes in additional consideration at that point. The options-based framework highlights the relevance of viewing incomplete DB pension contracts from a game theory perspective. When a win-win game switches to a win-lose game, players with stronger bargaining positions will extract balance sheet gains for their own purposes, and shift loses to weaker players.

- From a regulatory perspective, it is worthwhile distinguishing between 'short' and 'long horizon' solvency risk. Large 'Contingent Assets' values signal material solvency risk, especially if they are of a 'Musical Chairs' variety. However, this solvency risk could be either of a short horizon nature (e.g. the plan sponsor is an airline), or it could be of a long horizon nature (e.g. the pension plan is an industry fund such as PGGM or Ontario Teachers', which has zero default exposure in a short horizon context, but whose pension deal could ultimately still be unsustainable in a long horizon context). An interesting and important question here is: what are the optimal regulatory actions in these two cases? It would seem that in both cases the regulator should require the 'Musical Chairs' option values to be reduced to zero immediately. In other words, pension contracts should always be fully specified. However, the timing and mechanisms employed to rebalance the defined part of the balance sheet in the two cases might differ. These insights might help diffuse some of the regulatory 'Mexican stand-offs' that currently exist between regulators and funds in the pensions world.

One further implication of these insights is that it takes sophisticated organizations to measure, manage and explain the web of contingent claims embedded in any DB pension deal. While (in theory at least) DC-based pension deals do not have contingent claims, it still requires high effective organizations to create, communicate and manage a limited number of 'efficient' investment options, and to regularly report results to stakeholders.

3.6. Pension-delivery institutions

This leads to yet another 'Q&A' sequence about pension-delivery institutions:

Q: 'Are there effective pension-delivery institutions that can sort out these pension risk measurement and management issues, and that can cost-effectively deliver pension streams that meet the criteria of risk transparency developed above?'
A: 'No, but a few are seriously working on it'.

The sad truth is that much of the global 'pension industry' suffers from severe 'can't see the forest for the trees' problems. In other words, most pension people are so focused on their own pension tree, that they cannot even see the pension forest within their own organization, let alone the broader national or global pension forest. The 'tree' problem is especially serious with DB and DC plans in the corporate sector. Here the Human Resource department typically looks after benefits including pensions, the Treasury department typically looks after pension investments, and nobody (i.e., not the CFO, not the CEO, nor the Board) typically seems to be accountable for understanding and managing enterprise-wide pension risks. With such widespread organizational dysfunction in the corporate sector, we should not be surprised that few here are asking the ultimate pension questions behind the traditional DB and DC plan answers.

Industry/public sector pension funds are generally in a somewhat better position to ask ultimate pension questions. Why? Because they do not have to deal with the often-conflicting goals of having to create shareholder value on the one hand, and DB plan member value on the other. Having said that, industry/public sector funds are only now beginning to address the DB balance sheet risk measurement, management, and disclosure implications of moving to a 'fair value' framework. Nor has the actuarial profession been in the vanguard of change. It has been interesting to watch the debate between the minority in the actuarial profession advocating a move to a 'fair value' framework to assess DB plan solvency and funding requirements, and the majority who seem to want to carry on with the current ad hoc, 'rules of thumb'-based approach.

Does this organizational and professional dysfunction translate directly into ineffectiveness for today's traditional DB and DC plans as pension delivery vehicles? In other words, relative to the 'best practices' standards developed above, how do traditional DB and DC plans fare? Specifically, how effectively do current pension delivery mechanisms deal with pension adequacy, default risk, multiple employer risk, inflation risk, longevity/mortality risk, contribution rate risk and the broader questions of transparency, sustainability and organizational effectiveness? Table 3.1 tells the tale, at least the way we see it. The bottom line is clear. Neither of the traditional pension plan formulas scores particularly well when all eight benchmarking criteria are considered.

3.7. The way ahead

Can we design pension formulas and organizations that are more effective than those associated with the traditional DB and DC plans? Absolutely. The eight criteria listed in Table 3.1 show the way. Clearly, pension adequacy and portability are two important considerations. However, we believe that it is in the measurement, management and disclosure of the various kinds of risks embedded in 'pension deals' that the maximum scope for improvement lies.

*Table 3.1. **Benchmarking traditional DB and DC plan effectiveness***

	DB Plans	DC Plans
Pension adequacy	Good to moderate	Moderate to poor[1]
Contribution rate risk	High to moderate	High to low[2]
Default risk	Moderate to low	Low
Inflation risk	Moderate to low	High
Longevity/mortality risk	Low	High
Multiple employer risk	High to moderate	Low
Transparency	Poor	Good/poor[3]
Organizational effectiveness	Good to poor	Good to poor

[1]Investment regime risk, choice overload, inadequate savings risks, and high cost burdens are all problematic.
[2]In some corporate DC plans, employer contributions depend on profitability.
[3]Transparency in DC plans is generally good regarding account balances and poor regarding what pension those account balances will ultimately buy.

There is an important caveat of course. Material improvements in the measurement, management and disclosure of pension risks cannot occur without organizational structures willing and able to perform these tasks.

It is beyond the scope of this chapter to fully detail 'the way ahead'. Suffice it here to say that the interests of pension plan stakeholders are furthered best by pension delivery organizations that (1) are consciously structured to align the economic interests of the various stakeholder groups party to the pension deal, (2) have effective governance practices, (3) understand risk measurement and management, (4) have clear, defensible investment beliefs and (5) can dynamically integrate all of these factors to produce measurable value for their stakeholders over time [1]. However, none of these things is possible without first adopting a common 'fair value' foundation to measuring hard and contingent assets and liabilities. This is *'sine qua non'* of future progress in pension design and delivery.

Endnote

[1] This author has been a student of, and advocate for the articulation of 'best practices' in pension delivery organizations for many years. The first attempt to codify these 'best practices' resulted in the 1986 book 'Pension Funds and the Bottom Line'. A second, more complete attempt (with Don Ezra) resulted in the 1998 book 'Pension Fund Excellence: Creating Value for Stakeholders'. The writing of this chapter coincides with the launch of a new endeavour to fully describe and codify 'best practices' in the pension fund management field. Its intellectual foundation is *Integrative Investment Theory (IIT)*, which formally links five drivers of pension fund value-creation: (1) agency issues minimization, (2) effective governance, (3) relevant risk measurement and management, (4) defensible investment beliefs and (5) cost-effective integration/implementation. The development and implementation of *IIT* is the mission of the newly formed *Rotman International Centre for Pension Management* at the Rotman School of Management, University of Toronto. An article setting out the key elements and power of *IIT* ('Beyond Portfolio Theory: the Next Frontier') was published in a recent issue of the *Financial Analysts Journal*. The outline of a new *efficient personal pension accumulation model (EPPAM)* based on the behavioral finance and agency considerations set out above was recently sketched out by the author in a paper titled 'DB Plans Under Siege: Can They Survive?'.

Bibliography

Ambachtsheer, K. (1986), *Pension Funds and the Bottom Line*, Homewood, Illinois: Dow Jones Irwin.

Ambachtsheer, K. (2005), "Beyond portfolio theory: the next frontier", *Financial Analysts Journal,* January-February. Charlottesville, Virginia: CFA Institute.

Ambachtsheer, K. (2005), "DB Plans Under Siege: Can They Survive?" Discussion paper presented at the Rotman ICPM Workshop on Pension Plan Design, Risk and Sustainability, May 31–June 1, 2005, www.rotman.utoronto.ca/icpm.

Ambachtsheer, K. and D. Ezra (1998), *Pension Fund Excellence: Creating Value for Stakeholders*, New York: John Wiley & Sons Inc.

PART II

Technical

Fair Value and Pension Fund Management
N. Kortleve, T. Nijman and E. Ponds (Editors)
© 2006 Elsevier B.V.

CHAPTER 4

The Fair Value Principle

Jon Exley

4.1. Introduction

In this chapter we set out the basic economic principles behind fair values. The key arguments advanced in this chapter are:

1. The use of fair values is beneficial in terms of economic welfare because it helps individuals to make optimal decisions (or conversely, use of any other value leads to suboptimal decisions in a well functioning market economy).
2. Apparent obstacles to the use of fair values, such as the linkage of contracts to non-traded wage inflation, discretionary practices (conditional indexation) and default risk can be overcome without abandoning the main economic principles behind fair values.
3. Although the assumptions required for fair values to be an appropriate are likely to be met from the perspective of a shareholder looking at the economic cost of meeting pension and insurance liabilities, these assumptions are less likely to be met from the perspective of an individual beneficiary, for whom we argue a fair value generally represents an *upper bound* on the value.

The last of these arguments lays down an important challenge for the pensions and insurance industry.

4.2. Individual choices

Pension and insurance assets and liabilities do not exist in isolation – they are part of a wider economic framework. Individuals in this wider economy make many choices. Take, for example the choice between consuming now or saving for the future. Textbook economic theory suggests that in equilibrium an individual should be indifferent between a marginal dollar allocated to consumption or saving. Were this not the case then the individual could enhance his own well being by either saving more and consuming less or consuming more and saving less.

This concept does not stop at consumption and saving. Within the chosen consumption, individuals are in principle also marginally indifferent between spending an extra dollar on apples or oranges. Within their saving they should also be marginally indifferent between holding an extra dollar of equities or bonds etc. Thus even if individuals prefer a very high allocation of savings to equities and a low allocation to bonds or cash, they should not regard the last dollar allocated to equities as worth more than their last dollar allocated to bonds – both opportunities should be worth the same. If individuals wanted to allocate more than 100% of their wealth to equities then financial products, or securities, should be created to satisfy this desire. Indeed, such products already exist in an easily accessible form of exchange traded futures contracts.

We can go further than this – individuals should also allocate their time optimally (within the available opportunity set) between work and leisure. For example, they can choose to work hard today and save a lot so as to retire to a life of uninterrupted leisure from an early age, or they can work less hard today or save less with the aim of doing part-time work throughout some of their later life (this is of course a very pertinent analogy in the case of pensions where employers take it upon themselves to save on behalf of their employees). However, in a market economy it is all a matter of choices made within the available opportunity set – and based on market prices of labour, financial assets, consumer goods etc.

4.3. The wider economy

From the perspective of the wider economy it is also important to stress that individuals' demand for equities and bonds or apples and oranges does not take place in a vacuum. By expressing these individual, marginal, preferences the individuals collectively, through their aggregate demand, also affect prices. If the prices change as a consequence it may then affect preferences, and so on. Take for example, individuals' preferences for apples or oranges and suppose that there is a large supply of oranges due to a good harvest. If the price of oranges falls, then individuals may buy more oranges before they reach the point of marginal indifference between spending that extra dollar on apples or oranges. By increasing aggregate demand in response to the fall in price, fewer oranges will then rot in the fields – the individuals will feel better for having satisfied their desire for fresh fruit at a lower price and overall economic welfare will have been enhanced.

It is important to note that even though the vagaries of orange harvests mean that the price of oranges can vary, economic welfare is destroyed either by fixing orange prices or by forcing shoppers to decide on their weekly fruit intake without telling them the price that they are going to have to pay. In either case, the result would involve loss of welfare, the variable market price conveys important economic information. A similar conclusion would apply if employers took it upon themselves to buy a fixed quota of oranges for their employees every week – and the shops accordingly stopped selling them – welfare would again probably be destroyed.

Of course employers generally do not buy oranges for their employees, but they do buy them pensions.

4.4. Fair values in pensions and insurance

Valuations of pension and insurance contracts are performed for a variety of reasons, and often commissioned by agents (company management, trustees, government regulators) rather than the principals or 'end users' (shareholders of insurance companies or sponsoring companies, taxpayers, policy holders or pension scheme beneficiaries). However, from the perspective of these end-users there is only actually one important economic question that a valuation answers, namely 'what is the economic value of this financial contract' – by which we mean what is the value of the contract in the same currency that these individuals use to decide between apples and oranges or consumption and saving.

4.5. The Law of One Price

The key economic principle behind the application of this fair value approach in pensions and insurance is the Law of One Price. Although many critics of fair values will refer to market efficiency as the central (and strong) assumption behind fair values, the degree of reliance on efficient markets is often substantially overstated.

The Law of One Price is a fundamentally weaker assumption than efficient markets – in other words markets can be grossly inefficient (meaning that there are many opportunities for investors to derive abnormally high risk adjusted returns by adopting particular investment policies) whilst still obeying this law. All that is required for the law of one price to hold is that identical cashflows have the same value regardless of the legal structure delivering the cashflows. For example, if we hold $1 of equities in a unit trust and the payouts from this unit trust holding are identical to the payouts that one would obtain from holding the same $1 equities directly, then they both have a value – the fair value – of $1.

Of course, in this extreme form, the Law of One Price is of limited use – it is unlikely that we will ever be comparing two absolutely identical sets of cashflows in applying this law to pensions and insurance in practical situations. For example, the payments from a unit trust will probably not be *exactly* the same as the payments from holding the same assets directly – there may be expenses and various transaction costs and possibly taxation effects to take into account. The need to allow for these latter sorts of issues means that although efficient markets are not a central assumption behind fair values, a version of the efficient market theory is often required as a subsidiary assumption to fill in some gaps in practical applications. In other words, if two sets of cashflows only differ owing to some minor discrepancies then we need some way of pricing these discrepancies (or a reason to justify ignoring them). A good example of this in this context, a classical application of efficient markets would be to assert that if the risks associated with the discrepancies are 'non-systematic' then we can apply the same value to both cashflows, provided that the discrepancies have zero expectation.

If residual risks have a systematic component then we may need to use an asset pricing model (and associated model assumptions) to derive a reasonable adjustment to a fair value derived using the Law of One Price. However, it is important to stress that it is usually only at the margins that we need to make adjustments based on such models (although it is fair to say that most of the skill and expertise in valuation is associated with these adjustments). In general, the basic valuation of most pension and insurance liabilities by reference to easily recognisable comparables is rather easy – what is perhaps surprising is that we could have got this basic component of the valuation so wrong in the past.

4.6. Simple example

Let us therefore consider a simple application of the fair value principle using the Law of One Price in the context of defined benefit pensions. We will choose a contract for which an assumption of complete markets is reasonable and we will ignore transaction costs. We will also, perhaps, implicitly assume that individuals are rational and free of behavioural biases. These latter simplifying assumptions will be discussed below.

Suppose that a company sponsored pension scheme promises to pay an employee – or his estate, to remove the need for demographic assumptions initially – a lump sum of $100 in thirty years time. Suppose further that this promise is backed by a fund that is currently invested in cash deposits but these deposits are currently sufficient to cover *twice over* the cost of buying a thirty year zero coupon treasury bond paying $100 in thirty years time. Furthermore, a trustee (or a regulator) will ensure (daily) that if this level of cover falls below 200% then either the sponsoring company injects more cash immediately *or* the asset allocation is switched immediately from cash into thirty year zero coupon treasury bonds. Although commonly termed a pension fund, the assets here would be recognised in any other financial context as so called 'collateral' – set at twice the cost of hedging the liability with treasury bonds and subject to daily reset. In other words the liability is 'highly collateralised.'

What is the value of this highly collateralised promise to the employee and what is the cost of the promise to the sponsoring employer?

The Law of One Price says that, aside from default risk the value and cost of this benefit is the same as the price of a zero coupon thirty year treasury bond, because aside from default risk the pension payment is exactly the same as the payment from this bond. Although default is not impossible in this example (the price of zero coupon bonds could double over a single day, and the employer could simultaneously go bankrupt), the risk is negligibly small and (assuming some market regularity) the price of this risk is likely also to be negligibly small. To make this a concrete example, suppose the price of the matching zero coupon bond, and the fair value of the benefit promise, is $20.

The example is constructed in this contrived way to emphasise that the fund (or collateral) does not have to be invested in the zero coupon bond in order for the value of this contract to the employee (and the cost to the sponsor) to be the same as the price of the bond. The fund in this case is invested in cash. The price is the same because in just about every conceivable scenario (aside from bond prices doubling and the employer going bankrupt in a single day) the cashflows from the pension promise and from the bond are identical.

Although this fair value may be described as a 'modern' approach, it is in reality perhaps best described as 'neoclassical.' The economic justification for this approach may be more sophisticated in the modern context, but discounting liabilities using treasury interest rates is a very traditional actuarial approach. It does however contrast fundamentally with the actuarial practice of valuing a liability by discounting at the 'expected' return on the assets held in the fund – or asset and liability modelling studies which argue that the cost of liabilities can be directly reduced through choice of assets with higher expected returns (we return later to the issue of default risk associated with such assets).

4.7. Economic benefits of using the fair value – obligor's perspective

We can now explore some of the economic advantages of working with this 'fair value' of the contract. Let us look first from the perspective of a shareholder in the sponsoring employer (or a taxpayer if the employer is state owned) – in other words the obligor paying the benefit. Clearly this pension promise is a *liability* to this shareholder. If we suppose that the shareholder is entitled to receive any balance of the fund remaining after paying out the benefit then the economic liability to the shareholder is the same as if he had a short (sold) position in a thirty year treasury bond and a long position in cash deposits. In other words, since the cash deposits cover the liability twice over, the overall position of the shareholder is:

Short position in bond	$20
Long cash position	$40
Net asset	$20

The use of these fair values is correct to the extent that if the shareholder viewed these values differently – for example, if personally he thought that the bond was worth more (or less) than $20 then he should buy (or sell) these bonds at the open market price (of $20) until he reaches a point of indifference between spending (or receiving) another $1 on buying (selling) this asset or buying (or selling) any other asset. At this point the above fair values would once again apply.

Furthermore, it is clear that reporting a liability value of more or less than $20 to this shareholder would be at best unhelpful. We say 'at best' because in principle as long as the shareholder has enough information to value the liability himself (at fair value) he should not care what value he is told. However, in the absence of this information, if the shareholder is told that the liability is only $10 (for example by discounting using expected returns on equities, if the fund is switched into equities) then (absent other information) the value that he assigns to his shareholding may be erroneous. Such errors should not be taken lightly.

At the level of this $20 the mis-valuation associated with ignoring fair values is obviously trivial, but applied to a $20 billion pension liability the shareholder might mistake a badly managed company with high employment costs for a well-run company with low employment costs. As a result, capital may be allocated more cheaply to a badly managed company at the expense of a well-run company. This may mean that although a group of employees may continue to receive a more generous pension promise than would otherwise have been the case (if the liability had been reported to shareholders on a fair value basis), the misallocation of capital to a badly managed company ensures that the economic welfare is destroyed overall. Economic decisions being taken on mis-valuation of liabilities is simply an extension of our example or oranges rotting in the fields.

4.8. Economic benefits of using the fair value – obligee's perspective

The use of fair values is slightly more complex when viewed from the perspective of the other end user – the employee or obligee in receipt of a benefit. The additional complexity arises because in the case of a typical obligor (shareholder or taxpayer in the case of a state run industry) we can usually assume confidently that either the assets and liabilities represent marginal contributions to the obligor's total wealth (thus suggesting marginal indifference to the choice between various asset exposures) or (if the asset or liabilities represent a larger component of wealth) he is able to go long or short of his exposure using his other available asset portfolio. For example, in the example we gave above we assumed that he could buy or sell treasury bonds. However, in the case of an individual employee, it is likely that his pension is not a marginal component of his wealth but instead represents his single (or only) asset and whilst he may have proxies for shorting this pension benefit (the obvious example in the case of a thirty-year guaranteed cash benefit being a thirty-year mortgage) he may have limited ability to do so within his portfolio of other assets. This means that in our simple example the fair value of the promise is an *upper limit* on the value placed on the promise by the employee.

However, leaving aside this issue, we can see that the fair value remains relevant to the employee because it represents the amount of additional salary he would in this example (given that the benefit here is easily replicable) want as a substitute for the benefit promise. Given this amount of cash he could invest in a thirty-year treasury bond in a defined contribution pension arrangement and receive exactly the same benefit. Therefore, this fair value is the amount that company management should use in order to establish employee remuneration policy. Faced with this fair value choice (which is neutral to the obligor) the employee can allocate not only between investing $20 in bonds (with 'exactly' the same payout) or $20 in equities within a defined contribution plan, but the employee can also decide rationally between spending the $20 or saving – and in doing so make his marginal contribution to the equilibrium level of long term interest rates in the economy.

By contrast, it is clear that economic welfare is destroyed by encouraging the employee to save by offering him an 'off market' choice between the pension worth $20 (on a fair value basis) or an extra $10 of salary. There may be other economic costs associated with paying cash in lieu of pension benefits (such as free rider costs where the company is pressured into providing pensions for spendthrift employees – see Bodie and Merton (1993)), but these costs should be valued and justified explicitly and not simply used to justify an arbitrarily understated pension cost (for example by discounting at the expected return on equities). Economic welfare is after all maximised by individuals making rational choices – in particular between work and leisure, spending and saving. When (real) interest rates are low or people are expected to live much longer and defined benefits become expensive to in fair value terms then a rational economic response may be for employees to choose to defer retirement and work longer, rather than allocate an increasingly large proportion of their income to the purchase of an expensive defined benefit pension from an early age.

By using non-fair values in offering employees choice, these rational policy responses by individuals (e.g. working longer or accepting lower income in retirement) are discouraged – the overall consequence being detrimental, rather than beneficial, to the working of the economy. At worst, this use of non-fair values results in employees enduring the misery of low disposable income (excessively high forced saving) during their working life, when they would happily have accepted lower income in retirement (or later retirement) if given a choice based on fair values. Furthermore, shareholders may have paid excessively for labour (the employees may have settled for lower total compensation value if paid entirely in cash). The potential costs of such mis-valuation are non-trivial when applied on the scale of the pensions industry.

4.9. Complete markets, transaction costs and rational behaviour

We made a number of simplifying assumptions in our example above (or contrived an example where these assumptions were valid) leading to the key conclusion that the fair value represents an *upper bound* on the value of a financial contract given in lieu of cash salary to an individual beneficiary. Namely, we assumed that markets are complete and free of transaction costs and (implicitly) that individuals behave rationally. However, we do not see these assumptions as particularly strong in the context of our discussions here.

It is worth saying that markets are incomplete in many respects – there are lots of financial contracts which *do not* exist (infinitely more than the number of contracts which do exist). However this incompleteness is largely explained either by lack of demand for forms of contract which investors simply do not want or by the ability of existing contracts to replicate closely other possible types of contract within reasonable transaction cost bounds.

Thus for example, if pension schemes filled a vast chasm of demand for wage indexed financial products, we might expect to find that there was some residual demand from individuals for such contracts after some employed individuals had been given an un-tailored allocation to such a contract (via compensation) in the form of a standard accrual of pension benefit indexed to wages. We might also suppose that not all individuals with a strong demand for such a contract are able to find employment offering such benefits. We might also see pensions linked to wage indexation emerging in large market economies such as the US and UK (as discussed below the forms of defined benefit pensions generally seen in these economies are not indexed, in economic terms, to wage inflation). In normal circumstances this demand would also be expected to lead to companies (for example) seeing cheap financing costs associated with the issue of wage-linked bonds, or insurance companies issuing products linked to national average wage growth.

The fact that companies do not issue such bonds could be indicative of many underlying causes. For example it could be the case that, as with many other unavailable contracts, individuals simply do not want them, or it could be that the contracts are sufficiently replicable with existing tradable assets. Alternatively, it may be that the human resource departments of companies are more focussed on adding value through addressing market incompleteness opportunities than finance and treasury professionals. Whatever the explanation, we do not find the absence of complete markets a particularly convincing reason for the fair value of a wage indexed benefit substantially exceeding a naïve calculation of fair value by reference to existing tradable instruments. Furthermore, it is by no means obvious that a lack of a tradable asset similar to a particular financial product is a justification for valuing the contract at a premium to the most closely matching tradable – it may indeed justify valuing at a discount.

Transaction costs are, of course, also relevant in the context of the value placed by an individual on a benefit, but only if we establish that the individual wants the benefit in the first place (transaction costs work in the opposite direction if the individual wants to short the benefit). In addition we must apply transaction costs in an even-handed manner (i.e. also include the costs of providing the financial contract in question). Furthermore, sales and distribution costs are not only costs – economic benefits are derived from this expenditure – for example they ensure that financial products are bought by people who actually want them, which is worth bearing in mind. Thus again, although it may be appropriate to adjust the value of a financial contract for sales costs (for example), it may also be appropriate to adjust the value for an equal (or greater) cost associated with misallocation due to the absence of the sales process.

Finally, the assumption of rationality by individuals may be seen as strong or weak depending on one's view of behavioural biases. However, in the context of fair values we see no obvious way in which alternative methods of valuation can encompass irrational behaviour, nor even whether such biases should lead us to adopt a premium or discount to fair value in any practical application.

4.10. Valuation of linkage to wage inflation

A contract linked to wage inflation is, as discussed above, one obvious example of a lack of complete market for pension valuation purposes and the impact of a linkage between the liabilities and employee wages is often cited as a case where the straightforward calculation of fair values breaks down. There are however two distinct examples of pension liabilities linked to wage inflation:

(a) The 'final salary' nature of many pension liabilities;
(b) The provision for pensions (for example in the Netherlands) to increase in line with average wages.

The first of these linkages to wage inflation is in fact irrelevant in terms of the application of fair values. This is because the final salary linkage (in general) applies only while an employee remains in employment with the company sponsoring the pension scheme. As such the final salary link (in excess of the rate of escalation promised to a former employee) only accrues during employment. The value of this element of accrual is thus indistinguishable (in economic value terms) from the rest of an employee's compensation each year. Since the future compensation of employees does not form part of the economic pension liability today it is not part of the fair value calculation – only the benefit accrued by the employee if he left service at the valuation date represents the economic cost (and value) of the benefit accrued to date. This accrued value is based on current salary (plus either nil increases, retail price increases or national average wage increases pre-retirement) and not based on an individual's 'final salary.'

However, the salary link cannot be dismissed as easily in the second case above, where pension benefits are linked (either on early termination or in retirement) to national average wages. In these circumstances we are left with the problem of placing a fair value on a financial contract linked to average wages in the economy. The best way to approach this is to establish how we would hedge such a contract using traded financial instruments – if we can find the price of the best hedge then we have a good handle on the value of the contract.

Many commentators have supposed that there might be a link between equities and average wages on the basis of the general economic reasoning that both are potentially linked to general growth in the economy.

However, this common link with economic growth is specious for many reasons, to name but a few:

(a) The link between employee wages and economic growth is more strongly associated with *numbers* employed (total wages) rather than wages per employee (as measured by wage indices).
(b) The link between company profits and economic growth (if it exists) is more strongly associated with the growth in the number of firms (or returns on new capital investment) rather than growth in profits per share (as received by an equity investor).
(c) Even if aggregate profits and wages both increase with general economic growth, their proportions of gross domestic product vary – they represent returns to competing factors of production.
(d) Equities listed on a domestic market may derive a substantial proportion of their profits from abroad – and many employees in the economy comprising the wages index may be employed by overseas companies.
(e) The wage index may include a substantial proportion of public sector workers.
(f) The wages index is based on pre-tax income, whilst equity returns are based on post-tax income and are affected by tax changes.

Despite the lack of encouragement from this more considered analysis of the likely relationships, it is worthwhile to consider how we might construct a hedge for a wage indexed liability using equities. In order to establish such a quantitative hedge the first point to stress is that we need to compare like-with-like. For example we either need to:

(a) compare equity values with the value of a salary related asset or liability; or
(b) compare equity income (dividends or profits) with a salary index.

If we stick to this like-for-like comparison in statistical analysis then one immediate problem in any research is of course the available data. We have good data on equity prices, but no data on the market value of salary related assets or liabilities. On the other hand we have good data on wage indices but the data on equity income is less good. However, even after attempting to address these data issues the results may seem somewhat unexciting. For example, Smith (1998), who attempts to adjust in a sophisticated manner for the various lags in wage and dividend indices still finds that equities represent only a statistically insignificant 3% of the hedge for a liability linked to average wages, the rest of the hedge comprises nominal and inflation linked bonds.

Thus the principles of the fair value approach suggest that the value of an obligation linked to average wages is basically allowed for by starting with market implied inflation derived from price indexed bonds simply adding ones best estimate of the additional liability arising from wage inflation.

4.11. Discretion and conditional benefits

So the valuation of wage indexed liabilities is after all relatively straightforward. A more difficult aspect to allow for precisely is however, the effect of discretionary increases in benefits, or benefits linked to returns on the assets held. The difficulty here is not in the principle of how these should be valued, but rather in prescribing the rules under which the benefits will be calculated in these circumstances. This difficulty in turn suggests that although the cost to the obligor may be well represented by a fair value approximation, the value to the obligee of non-transparent and ill-defined benefits is likely to be substantially less than this fair value (once again the fair value represents an upper bound on the value to individual recipients of the benefit).

The simplest case to consider (and thus the case likely to destroys least value) is where an employee benefit can be expressed as a simple linear combination of a defined benefit (which van be valued as a bond as discussed above) plus the returns on a defined contribution 'pot' belonging to the employee. This type of structure has clear and unambiguous value and cost to all parties. The defined benefit has a clear cost to the sponsor and value to the employee and the defined contribution pot has a value to the employee (give or take the effect of transaction costs and expenses) equal to its current market value, with no contingent liability to the sponsor regardless of the asset allocation of this pot. The value of benefit can simply be expressed as a linear combination of the value of a bond plus the value of the asset pot.

The transparency of this 'linear' structure means that all parties can have clear and transparent information about their economic exposures, which allows them to make rational economic decisions and in principle ensures that economic welfare is maximised.

The situation is slightly different if we consider more complex, non-linear, linkage between the assets of a pension fund and its liabilities. For example suppose that the fund provided average wage indexation of benefits only if the fund returns achieve certain levels. If this contract is fully specified then it

can be represented as an asset to employees equivalent to a national average
wage inflation linked bond *less* the value of a put option on the fund. Equivalently, as a liability the shareholders of the company are short of this bond
but long of the put option asset. This fair value approach therefore reveals an
important truth – although presented as a form of 'risk sharing' all that matters to the shareholders in this context is the amount of 'cost sharing.' In other
words all that is important to the shareholder is the amount of cost saved by
the value of the put option, relative to the cost of full wage indexation.

Once again from our economic framework we find that sharing 'risks' is
generally of no value to the obligor. If we are looking at marginal parts of the
obligor's total portfolio then this indifference to risk exposure is axiomatic.
However, even if we are looking at economy-wide practices in all corporate pension plans (which may then have a significant impact on the risk
characteristics of an equity portfolio), once shareholders (for example) are
aware of the rules governing the contingent payments from pension plans,
the asset risk exposures they incur can in principle be hedged by adjusting
other items of their personal portfolios so as to recover their preferred asset
exposures.

From this shareholders perspective the worst structure is an imprecise link
between the fund returns and the contingent liabilities, since they cannot then
know what their overall asset exposures are, nor can they value employment
costs in companies accurately (with associated economic costs as discussed
earlier). Once the link is prescribed they simply have exposure to a put
option asset – and they are indifferent to the underlying risk exposure of this
put, caring only about its value provided that they can readjust their other
assets to remove any unwanted asset risks.

From the employees' perspective, the value of discretionary practices
such as this are less clear. As with the shareholder, the employee will suf-
fer a cost associated with lack of transparency if the benefit is not clearly
defined – since the employee will be unsure of both the economic value
of the benefit and the risk characteristics, leading to potentially suboptimal
savings, consumption and asset allocation decisions by the individual.

However, the employee may be at the added disadvantage of being
unable to hedge a complicated form of contingent benefit. The argument
that the obligor sees only the value of the put option and is indifferent to the
underlying risk exposures does not apply symmetrically to the obligee. For
example, whereas we argued that it may be possible for many employees
to short unwanted exposure to a simple bond (via mortgage borrowing for
example) it is far less easy for an employee to take a short position in a

complicated contingent claim on the equity market via a company pension benefit. This means that although the economic cost of the liability to the obligor may be assessed by reference to traded assets, the employee could in principle place a much lower value than this on a complicated contingent pension benefit that forms a large proportion of his total wealth.

4.12. Default risk

Finally, in terms of departures from our original simple example of applying fair value principles, we should note that our original simple example deliberately constructed a situation of a highly collateralised pension promise where the risk of default was minimal. The valuation of the default risk is however in principle another relatively straightforward application of fair value methods and is yet another example where (default) risk sharing is simply a misnomer for cost sharing.

To the extent that employees bear the risk of default this is a cost to employees (which can be valued as a put option on the value of the firm) and of value to the shareholder or obligor. As with the example of discretion above, if the rules of the funding of the plan can be defined accurately then the value of this option to default is relatively straightforward from the shareholder perspective – they are either marginally indifferent to, or able to diversify, the asset risk exposures associated with this option (which can be replicated by short positions in corporate debt). Once again they are then concerned only with the value of the option to default.

The value of this option is primarily determined by the level of funding of a pension plan – the easiest way to increase the value of the option to default is by holding less assets in the plan than required to secure the liabilities using treasury bonds. A secondary way of increasing the value of the option to default is by investing in assets (such as equities) that are likely to be negatively correlated with the value of the firm.

However, the extent to which shareholders can in practice exploit the value of this option by increasing the risk of default is constrained by:

(a) the extent to which employees can respond by demanding higher wages to compensate for the risk of pension default;
(b) the extent to which the actuary (or other party responsible for funding policy) insists on full funding of the liabilities;
(c) the requirements of regulators.

The employee perspective is largely a repeat of our previous comments – not only will employees find this option to default difficult to value without transparent information, but in this case the employee will almost certainly place a higher cost on the option to default than the value assessed by the shareholders. This is because employees will generally have limited ability to short their personal exposure to the fortunes of their employer and will be particularly averse to the joint risk of losing their job (through employer bankruptcy) and their pension (through default). Thus from the employees' perspective, bearing risk of default appears to be a highly inefficient means of reducing the cost of the benefit to the shareholders – the reduction in the value of the benefit to the employee arising from this risk seems to far outweigh the cost reductions to shareholders in a fair value framework. Once again therefore, the fair value calculated by reference to the economic value to a shareholder of the option to default probably represents an upper bound on the value of the benefit to the beneficiary.

4.13. The challenge of fair values: why buy pensions and not groceries?

By way of summary fair values generally represent a very good approximation to the cost of a liability to a provider of financial products like pensions. However, although fair values can be criticised on a number of grounds (or due to strong assumptions) in the case of the value of the benefit to the recipient, we find that in most cases these criticisms would lead us to see the fair value as an upper bound. The challenge thrown down by the use of fair values in the case of pension funds is therefore to explain the 'missing' value of pension provision by employers.

On the face of it, this challenge arising from the application of market value principles is not surprising. After all employers do not buy groceries for their employees, they instead tend to pay cash wages and let the employees do their own shopping. However, employers do take it upon themselves to effectively take cash out of employee pay packets and buy them a pension instead – it would be surprising if this added economic value in a straightforward way.

Furthermore, it would seem that the more complex the benefit and the more difficult it is for the employee to 'short' or sell unwanted exposure, the more value is destroyed. This suggests that far from adding value, complex benefits – for example involving inter-generational cross subsidy or imprecise contingent benefits – actually destroy more value than simple straightforward contracts.

4.14. Conclusions

The economic principles behind fair values are very simple – we find traded assets that replicate the same cashflows in order to value a financial contract. This approach relies most heavily on the Law of One Price – our key principle and we only need to assume regular or efficient markets in the valuation of discrepancies between the tradable assets and the contract in question.

The main gain from the use of fair values is transparency – the value of contracts is expressed in the same currency as we make all other economic decisions. The resulting welfare gains in terms of better economic decisions by individuals should not be understated, especially given the scale of pension liabilities in many countries and the extent of confusion over valuation hitherto.

We reject the idea that substantial gains relative to fair values can be recognised due to incomplete markets or transaction costs. Furthermore, overall both of these aspects have potential to argue for values seen by beneficiaries to be at a discount, rather than premium, to simple fair values based on existing traded assets.

Although the theory is most easily applied to plain vanilla defined benefits, the principles are the same for more complex benefits. Furthermore, in many cases – such as the inclusion of demographic risks, linkage with price inflation and wage inflation we argue that the principles are still very simple to apply. The supposed complexities associated with wage inflation linkage in particular are, we argue, often over stated.

Linking the benefit payments to the returns on the fund may add greater complexity (if the link is non-linear) but so called 'risk sharing' is in a fair value framework just a misnomer for cost sharing. Generally the obligors do not need to share risks as they can already diversify. In our view the obligees would however be likely to find such contracts non transparent, difficult to value and difficult to incorporate into optimal personal asset exposures. Default risk is similarly difficult to value and likely to be an unwanted exposure from an obligee's perspective and likely to result in beneficiaries valuing benefits at a discount to fair value.

The puzzle presented by fair values is why certain types of pension arrangements continue to persist despite their apparent destruction of value.

References

Bodie, Z. and R.C. Merton (1993), "Pension benefit guarantees in the United States: A functional analysis"; Chapter 5 in Schmidt R. ed, *The Future of Pensions in the United States*, University of Pennsylvania Press.

Smith, A.D. (1998), "Salary Related Cashflows; Market Based Valuation": paper presented to Institute of Mathematics and its Applications, available at http://www.gemstudy.com/DefinedBenefitPensionsDownloads/Salary_Related_Cash _Flows_Market_Based_Valuation.pdf.

Fair Value and Pension Fund Management
N. Kortleve, T. Nijman and E. Ponds (Editors)
© 2006 Elsevier B.V.

CHAPTER 5

Techniques for Market-Consistent Valuation of Contingent Claims

John Hibbert, Steven Morrison and Craig Turnbull (Barrie & Hibbert)

Keywords: market-consistent, risk-neutral, deflators

JEL codes: G12, G13

5.1. Background

A once-in-a-lifetime change to pension fund valuation practice is now taking place. Pension practitioners, corporate sponsors, pension fund trustees and regulators must now get to grips with the ideas behind so-called 'market-consistent' valuation methods. Implementation of the new thinking presents significant challenges for all involved.

This chapter aims to do two things for the reader and is split into two parts. First, to explain the central concept behind the market-consistent approach – the idea that many pension liabilities share common characteristics with traded financial assets and that these market prices can be used to put a sensible price on pensions liabilities. We contrast this with the traditional approach to valuation which – we argue – sets out to answer an entirely different question. Our second task is to show how the basic concept can be extended to value more complex types of liability. We illustrate, using simple numerical examples, how a framework can be developed to value *any* contingent claim. These ideas lie at the heart of the new market-consistent methods. Researchers and practitioners have extended the basic concepts to value more complex claims. Other chapters in this book explain some of these extensions.

5.2. Part I: Market-consistent methods – the basic idea

Let us begin with an example. Our objective is to give the reader some basic intuition for the ideas behind market-consistent valuation methods.

5.2.1. Introduction

Suppose that you own an inflation-protected bond that sells for £1000. An expert offers to buy it from you for £750. He tells you: *'if you invest the £750, in equities, you can expect (on average) to receive the same benefits as provided by the bond'*. Do you:

(a) Accept the offer. Experts surely know about these things. Besides, you do believe in the law of averages.
(b) Decline the offer. Why sell an asset that is worth £1000 at a 25% discount! You might argue: 'Surely, investing in equities will expose me to risk?'

If you chose answer (b) you should be particularly wary of traditional pension fund valuations. The calculations used in these valuations use principles that put a £750 value on your £1000 asset.

We would be the first to admit that this is a strange state of affairs, so let us explain how this has happened in more detail.

5.2.2. A case study

Let us illustrate our arguments with an example. Consider a hypothetical saver. Let us call him 'Frank'. He is offered a choice between a specified pension benefit and a pot of savings that can be invested with the objective of buying a pension. Frank is aged 50 and will draw a pension at the age of 60. He has a right to a pension of £15,000 pa that is protected against inflation. In other words, the initial pension will rise in line with inflation over the next 10 years until Frank's 60th birthday, then inflation increases will be granted (to protect purchasing power) until he eventually dies. Let us also assume that the pension is guaranteed for 5 years and there is a 50% pension for Frank's wife if he dies before her. Since the pension fund offering the pension is reckoned to be solvent and the sponsoring company is financially strong, the promised pension benefits are very secure.

This is a valuable asset. Frank has no need to worry about investment returns, inflation surprises or unexpected changes in mortality rates or interest rates. Frank owns a special sort of inflation-protected bond with cash flows that match the outflows we would project for a very large group of similar 50-year-olds. The anticipated cash flows are shown in Figure 5.1.

You might ask: *'Is there a market value for this bond?'* Of course, this sort of bond is not traded, but some very similar instruments are. Consider Figure 5.2. It shows the cost of buying an inflation-protected £1 for different future periods. You can see that if someone wants to acquire £1 of real purchasing power in 20 years time, the cost today is £0.637. We can express these prices as interest rates for each term. These are plotted in Figure 5.3. The equivalent real interest rate for 20 years is 2.26% (Figure 5.3). Now, if the cash flows required to pay Frank's deferred pension are each priced using the bond prices shown then added up, a price for the pension can be calculated of £18.14 per £1 of deferred inflation-protected pension.[1,2]

Figure 5.1.   *Projected real annuity cash flows for a deferred pension (60-year-old retiring in 2011 with 5 year guarantee and 50% Spouse's Pension)*

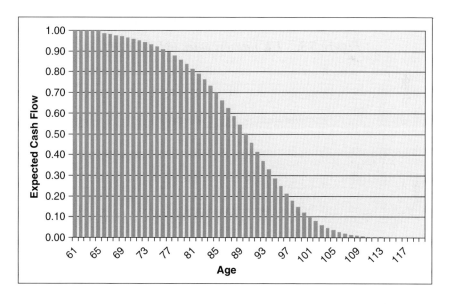

---

[1]We have assumed the pension will be paid monthly and allowed 4% for expenses.
[2]All calculations are shown to 3 significant figures.

Figure 5.2. Real discount bond prices (31 July 2001)

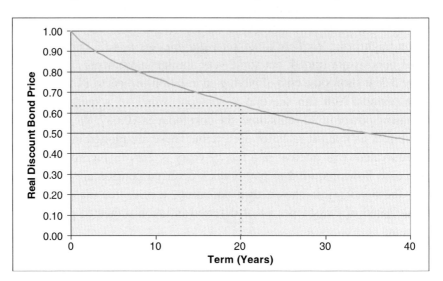

Figure 5.3. UK interest rates (31 July 2001)

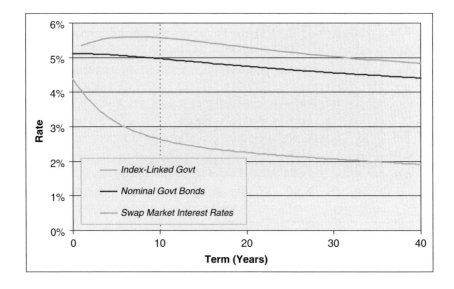

Since he has a right to a pension of £15,000 pa in today's money, his financial claim (the pension) is worth $15,000 \times 18.14 = £272,000$.

We reckon this is a good approximation for the market value of the pension. In other words, if Frank wanted to *buy* this benefit, £272,000 represents a good estimate for the likely cost. However, there are some comments we should make. First, the financial claim is exposed to some credit risk. In other words, there is a possibility that the pension fund could default on the claim and fail to meet its liabilities. In the analysis presented this risk is assumed to be very small. Credit risk will reduce the value of the pension asset. Second, the pension asset is not so easily tradable as an index-linked government bond. Someone might argue that some allowance should be made for this. Third, Figure 5.1 shows us what can be *expected* to be paid – on average – over a 60-year period by the pension fund. Of course, the pension fund will not pay £0.50 to anyone in year 30. It will pay £1 to one-half of the cohort of 60-year-olds who began drawing a pension at the same time as Frank. The other half are expected to have died. This projection is made using an actuary's estimate for the rate of future mortality. It turns out that actuaries have been quite poor at forecasting future mortality (because it is very difficult to forecast). This means that the pension fund (on which Frank owns a financial claim) must bear the risk that the actual mortality rate in the future is different from today's forecast. It could be argued that the inflation-protected (and mortality-risk-protected) claim is worth more than £272,000 because of this. Again we have ignored this effect even though it lends further weight to our arguments. Let us now understand how traditional actuarial practice puts a lower value on Frank's financial claim. To be fair, the actuarial approach sets out to answer *a different question*. However, there is a problem because both actuaries and their clients often fail to understand the difference between the two questions. The task of accumulating assets (stocks, shares and property) to pay a future pension suggests an alternative question: '*how much money does Frank need today in order to meet the pension liability?*' Let us see how the actuaries have set about answering this question.

Frank's pension of £15,000 is protected against inflation so that in 10 years time – assuming that inflation will average 2.75% pa – it is expected to have risen to $15,000 \times 1.0275^{10} = 19,675$ pa.[3] The actuary now uses a mortality table to project the cash flows to be paid (on average)

---

[3] In practice, inflation protection is capped. We have ignored the effect of the cap in our calculations. We believe that the existence of the cap does not make a material impact on our calculation or arguments.

to a 60-year-old. Instead of assuming *real* cash flows and discounting using a real interest rate, he typically uses nominal cash flows and discounts at a nominal interest rate. A typical assumption might be to inflate the cash flows at a rate of 2.75% pa (for inflation) then discount at a rate of 5.8% pa. Notice that the difference between these two rates is 2.97% pa and represents the *real* rate of interest implied by the assumptions.[4] You should note that this is somewhat higher than the real interest rates shown in Figure 5.3. The sum of discounted projected cash flows under this method is £20.0 per £1 of annuity. Since a pension of £19,675 pa is to be paid, a fund of 19,675 × 20.0 = 393,000 must be available at year 10. So how much is required *today* to deliver £393,000 in 10 years? Well, the discount functions derived from the government bond and swap markets should give us a pretty good idea. A discount government bond which pays £1 after 10 years will cost around £0.609. A comparable instrument from the swap markets costs £0.573. Contrast this with the discount factor used in a typical valuation calculation which is 0.528, equivalent to an annual rate of return of 6.6%. The actuary argues that, if the fund used to meet the pension is invested in a mixture of equities and bonds, a higher rate of return can be expected. This is because, on an average, equities can be expected to deliver a higher rate of return than risk-free investments. The actuary applies the discount factor to the required fund (at year 10) of £393,000 to give a required fund today £393,000 × 0.528 = £208,000. Note that this is nearly 25% lower than the market value we calculated for Frank's claim of £272,000. How can this be? Both numbers cannot be correct?

The difficulty and confusion arises because the two numbers tell us completely different things. The market value of £272,000 gives us the cost of *replicating* the benefits today (although we have suggested that the cost could be higher as we have not priced the mortality risk in such a contract). The value is *consistent with the market* price of government bonds. The lower actuarial value of £208,000 simply tells us what size of fund would be required to give an *expectation* (in the statistical sense only) of buying the pension benefits. Note that if Frank were to choose this route he would give up protection against a number of risks:

- Investment returns could be lower than 6.6% pa over the next 10 years. Adding fund expenses, the target is probably closer to 8% pa. This

---

[4]This is calculated as 1.058/1.0275 − 1 = 0.0297.

probability is significant – in the region of 55% for underperforming a rate of return of 8% over 10 years for a balanced fund.

- There is a risk that long – term interest rates in 10 years time could be lower than 5.8%. Indeed, today's forward bond yields are much lower than this – 4.5% for government bonds and 5.0% in the swap market. The expectation that long-term interest rates return to a 'normal' level of 5.8% may be quite reasonable (depending on who you talk to), but it is only a *view* and is subject to a high degree of error.
- There is a chance that rates of mortality could decline faster than is currently forecast by actuaries so that annuity rates (and pensions) are lower than forecast. You should note that there is a wide range of views among actuaries on the rate of future mortality improvement.
- Surprising inflation can affect the pension purchasing power of the pension.

The remarkable thing about the pension asset owned by Frank is that it provides protection against all of these risks. One of the main reasons the market value is so much higher than the actuarial funding value is because the market attaches value to these risks. If you bear a risk you normally expect to be compensated in some way. Insurance is not free. If I want to acquire an asset that pays £1 *for sure* in 10 years time, I can find out the price by reading off the curve in Figure 5.3. The actuarial present value of 0.528 simply tells me how much I should invest in equities to expect – on an average – to receive £1 after 10 years. As investors in Japanese equities know, this is far from certain.

5.2.3. Conclusion

Where does all of this leave us? Two quantities have been calculated. One is an estimate for the market value (replacement cost) of the pension asset. The second (actuarial) quantity could be helpful when we want to understand *funding* requirements, but we should be clear that it is not a *value*. The difficulty with the use of this quantity in pensions valuation calculations is that this difference is not apparent to most people. Anyone accepting the traditional valuation under the illusion that they are being fairly compensated for the rights they forego may be sorely disappointed. It can be difficult to look through the apparent complexity to a few key assumptions that can have a huge impact on 'actuarial values'.

Is Frank's situation really any different to the one outlined at the beginning of this essay? We do not think so. Although there is lots of detail in the traditional pensions calculations, the principles applied are exactly as set out in the question we posed in the introduction. There is a world of difference between the fair (market) value of an asset and a funding amount. When a person is offered a payment in exchange for giving up rights that they own, it seems reasonable to expect them to be offered fair value. This is *not* what the traditional approach offers them. Actuaries have had a grizzly time over the past few years because of their inability to measure, manage and price risk. There is now a growing awareness of the importance of market values within the actuarial profession. Our task in part II of this chapter is to explain some of the details of implementation of these methods when they are applied to more complex financial assets and liabilities.

5.3. Part II: Market-consistent valuation methods

5.3.1. Introduction

In part I we discussed the valuation of known (nominal or real) pension liabilities, where the value can be inferred from the prices of nominal and index-linked government bonds.[5] In practice, pension liabilities may not be directly observable in this way. For example, under conditional indexation schemes liabilities are contingent on the performance of some financial assets. How can we value these more general contingent claims?

Valuation of contingent claims presents some significant challenges. However, a major breakthrough in contingent claims pricing was made by *Black, Scholes and Merton* in 1973 and a vast literature on the pricing of a wide range of contingent claims has been developed since. Much of this work has been applied by practitioners to the management of financial assets and liabilities with embedded options. A ready-made library of tools and techniques now exists for actuaries and accountants who set out to measure fair values. At the heart of the modern literature lies the technique of *risk-neutral pricing*. Risk-neutral methods have been widely applied by practitioners in the banking industry to the pricing and hedging of contingent claims. An alternate mode of implementation of pricing models involves the use of *state price deflators* to calculate contingent claim values. In this section we discuss

---

[5]Ignoring credit risk and assuming that future mortality rates are perfectly forecast.

both valuation methods, and show that they are equivalent in the sense that they give rise to the same prices. We will illustrate our arguments by developing a series of examples based on binomial trees. Sections 5.3.3–5.3.5 illustrate the basic principles behind the two approaches to pricing using some simple 'binominal' examples.

5.3.2. Objectives and background

New accounting standards mean that – over the next few years – actuaries and accountants must develop a market-consistent framework for the valuation of the liabilities of life and pension funds. Whilst there are likely to be many technical challenges faced by those responsible for implementation, one of the most awkward areas relates to the valuation of options and other claims which are contingent on future underlying asset prices.

Options can be seen in many places – in financial markets, in markets for real assets as well as in everyday life. Options on financial assets are traded on financial exchanges everyday. You can read the price of this sort of option in the financial newspapers. Options are bought and sold by financial institutions as part of their day-to-day investment business. They usually appear on the asset side of a life company's balance sheet. Far more important are the options that might appear on the other side of a life company balance sheet. Consider three examples:

- Option to exchange cash benefits of a savings contract for pension at a rate of £10 fund/£1 pension.
- Option to exchange 'asset share' for a guaranteed amount on a pre-specified date.
- Option to surrender a term assurance contract and renew at a lower premium level.

These kinds of options have all been provided (i.e., written) by insurance companies and pension funds over the past few decades. The first is an annuity option of the type that has caused European insurers so many problems in recent years. In this case, when the option is exercised, the asset given by the option holder is his rights specified in terms (typically) of a with-profits fund value. The asset received is a pension at a pre-specified rate. The second option forms part of a 'plain vanilla' with-profits endowment contract that provides a guarantee in the form of sum assured and reversionary bonus. The final example concerns the implicit option a holder of a term assurance contract is granted – to surrender and to take out a replacement contract if mortality rates move in the policyholder's favour.

You cannot read the prices of these options in the financial newspapers. Transactions and 'open interest' are not reported. Yet, it is important to appreciate that large exposures do exist on the books of life assurance companies. Insurers write huge volumes of options exposure every day. They are in the business of selling options embedded in a wide range of business. What is astonishing, given the scale of these exposures, is that options know-how is still viewed by some actuaries as remote from their everyday work. In reality, understanding, pricing and managing options exposures is fundamental to actuarial work and the management of an insurance company or pension fund. Option pricing theory offers a set of tools for dealing with options.

Before we review the basic idea behind option pricing theory, let us say something about models in general. It is important to remember that a model is a cut-down, simplified version of reality that captures essential features and aids understanding. By simplication, you can see that a good model does not need to capture all real-world complexity in order to be useful. In our view the best models are parsimonious (simple), transparent (easy to understand) and evolve (you can add more complexity later if it is really necessary). One of the things that is so remarkable about the Black–Scholes–Merton (BSM) model is that practitioners would tell us that it does all of these things. Moreover, no practitioner (that we have ever met) believes that the model's assumptions actually hold in reality.

Let us now take a look at the basic (yet elusive) ideas behind option pricing methods and then examine pricing methods implemented using state price deflators.

5.3.3. Key insights of Black, Merton and Scholes

5.3.3.1. A basic binomial example

The key insights into the pricing of options that were developed more than 25 years ago by Fisher Black and his collaborators can be demonstrated using a simple binomial model for asset prices. Although the binomial model might not seem very impressive, it generates some valuable insights and (perhaps surprisingly) it can be extended to analyse real-world problems.

In order to illustrate the issues, we will begin by considering a risky asset whose price today is 100. You can think of the asset as an equity share.

Now, suppose that, one year from now, the share price can take on two possible values. Either it moves up to a level of 125, or down to 80:

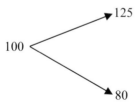

It is also assumed that it is possible to borrow and lend at a risk-free interest rate of 5%.

Now, suppose that we are offered a call option on the share with strike price $K = 102.5$. The buyer of this option has the right (but no obligation) to buy the share for 102.5 at the end of the year. How much should we be prepared to pay for such an option? To answer this question, we start by calculating the value of the option for each of the two possible outcomes. Suppose the share price moves up to 125. We have an option to buy the share at a lower price (102.5). The option is therefore worth 22.5 in this state (the difference between the share price and the option strike price). On the other hand, if the share price moves down to 80 the option is worthless – why buy something at 102.5 when you can get it elsewhere for 80? So, we know the value of the option in the two possible future states of the market:

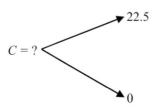

Now consider the following trading strategy:[6]

1. Buy half a share for 50; and
2. Borrow 40/1.05 to be paid back (with interest at 5%) at the end of the period.

---

[6]For simplicity, we assume that we can trade in arbitrary amounts of shares and cash without incurring transaction costs, taxes etc.

We can calculate the value of this portfolio in each future state. If the share price moves up, the share holding is worth $125/2 = 62.5$; if it moves down the share holding is worth $80/2 = 40$. In each case we will pay back the loan of 40 and hence the total value of the portfolio is:

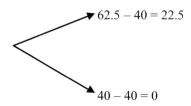

Note that the portfolio is worth exactly the same as the call option whatever happens to the share price. This special combination of assets is a *replicating portfolio* for the option. The portfolio replicates the option's payoffs for each possible final asset price. Since we know the current share price, we know the current value of this replicating portfolio: it is worth $(50/2) - (40/1.05) = 11.90$. And since the portfolio replicates the call option payoff in both future states, its current value must equal the current value of the option. The call option is therefore worth 11.90.

This result follows from the *law of one price*: if two assets generate the same cash flows in all future states of the world, they must be worth the same today. Why should this be the case? If it were possible to buy the call for less than 11.90 someone could sell the replicating portfolio for 11.90, buy the call option at the lower price and pocket the difference. This strategy gives a positive initial cash flow (the difference between the two prices) but zero net cash flows in both future states of the world. Similarly, if someone was prepared to pay us more than 11.90 for the option we should sell the option and buy the replicating portfolio. Either way it would be possible to get something for nothing. In general, we refer to such opportunities as examples of *arbitrage*. Economists generally like to assume that arbitrage opportunities do not exist. In reality, practitioners normally view them as fleeting, temporary opportunities usually only available to a specialised group of market participants.

Notice that we did not need to specify the probability of price changes in order to find the option price. The option value can be replicated by holding a portfolio of stock and cash and this portfolio depends only on the value of the stock and cash in each of the two future states, not on their probability.

5.3.3.2. *Generalising the single period example*

A specific example of pricing a call option in a one-step binomial market has been analysed. In this section we generalise the ideas presented in the example to the valuation of general contingent claims in the one-step binomial model. The market consists of a risky asset (stock) S and a risk-free asset (cash) B:

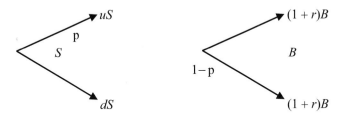

In this simple model, the risky asset will either increase in value to uS with probability p, or decrease in value to dS with probability $1 - p$. The risk-free asset, by definition, grows at the risk-free interest rate r regardless of the outcome.

Suppose a contingent claim (derivative) exists that pays V_{up} in the up-state and V_{down} in the down-state:

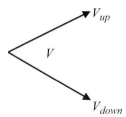

How might a fair price for this derivative be determined? From the simple numerical example in the previous section, you might guess that we should look for a portfolio of the stock and cash that perfectly replicates the derivative payoff. The portfolio consisting of Δ units of S and Ψ units of B evolves as follows:

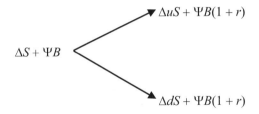

By equating the value of the portfolio with the value of the derivative in each of the two possible future states, the appropriate portfolio to match the two possible contingent claim values can be determined:

$$\Delta = \frac{V_{\text{up}} - V_{\text{down}}}{(u - d) S} \tag{5.1}$$

$$\Psi = \frac{1}{B(1 + r)} \left(V_{\text{up}} - \Delta u S \right) \tag{5.2}$$

Since this portfolio perfectly replicates the payoff of the derivative in both future states, its current value must equal the current value of the derivative. Any other price would present an arbitrage opportunity. Hence the fair price of the derivative is $V = \Delta S + \Psi B$. Inserting the above specification of Δ and Ψ we find, after some algebraic rearrangement:

$$V = \frac{1}{1 + r} \left[q V_{\text{up}} + (1 - q) V_{\text{down}} \right] \tag{5.3}$$

where q is defined:

$$q = \frac{(1 + r) - d}{u - d} \tag{5.4}$$

Notice that Equation (5.3) has a simple interpretation. We imagine a world in which assets move up with 'probability'[7] q. In this world, Equation (5.3) tells us that the expected return on all assets (including the stock S) is the risk-free rate. In this imaginary world investors earn the risk-free rate regardless of the riskiness of the assets they hold. For this reason q is sometimes called a risk-neutral probability and this method of pricing derivatives is called *risk-neutral pricing*.

Some people find it counter-intuitive to use a risk-free discount rate when pricing a risky asset, believing that it implies that the investor is not compensated for bearing risk. However, it turns out that there is no contradiction. The expectation for asset payoffs is calculated using the risk-neutral probability q and not the real-world probability p. In fact, the price of a derivative

---

[7]Note that, for the model to be arbitrage-free we require $d < 1 + r < u$ i.e., the share outperforms cash in one state and underperforms in the other. This in turn implies that $0 < q < 1$, and hence q can be interpreted as a probability (though we stress that this does not mean that it is the real world probability of an up-move).

is independent of the real-world probability p. Remember that we did not use the probability to derive the option value. To price a derivative we find its replicating portfolio, and this replicating portfolio does not depend on the probabilities attached to each state.

However you choose to interpret Equation (5.3), there is no doubt that it gives the unique no-arbitrage price of a derivative. And it does so in an efficient way. Once we have calculated the risk-neutral probability q, it is easy to value any derivative.

Example:

Consider our previous example. Here we have $r = 0.05, u = 1.25, d = 0.8$, so that the risk-neutral probability is $q = 5/9$. For the specific example of a call option with strike 102.5, we have $V_{\text{up}} = 22.5, V_{\text{down}} = 0$ and hence:

$$C = \frac{1}{1.05} \times \left[\frac{5}{9} \times 22.5 + \frac{4}{9} \times 0\right] = 11.90$$

This is the same result derived in Section 5.3.1 by explicitly calculating the replicating strategy.

5.3.3.3. Expectation pricing

The method for pricing derivatives described above is similar to the traditional actuarial practice of pricing assets by calculating their expected future value and discounting at a 'risk-adjusted' rate, reflecting the additional expected return demanded by investors for bearing risk. However Equation (5.3) discounts at the risk-free rate, regardless of the riskiness of the asset being priced and the expected value is calculated using the probability q, not p.

Suppose instead that we adopt the actuarial approach and estimate derivative prices by calculating expected future values under the real-world probability p, and discounting using a risk-adjusted discount factor. Equation (5.3) can be re-written as:

$$V = D_V \left[pV_{\text{up}} + (1-p)V_{\text{down}}\right] \tag{5.5}$$

where D_V is a risk-adjusted discount factor appropriate to the derivative:

$$D_V = \left(\frac{qV_{up} + (1-q)V_{down}}{pV_{up} + (1-p)V_{down}} \right) \times \frac{1}{1+r} \qquad (5.6)$$

Obviously, Equations (5.5) and (5.6) are just an inefficient way of writing Equations (5.3) and (5.4), but they may help clarify the point made in the previous section that no-arbitrage pricing is perfectly consistent with a world of risk-averse investors (provided $p > q$). Also, note that the discount factor D_V is specific to the derivative being valued. For example, the discount factor for a call option is different from that of the underlying stock.

Example:

Consider our previous example with the additional assumption that the real-world probability of the share price increasing is $p = 0.7$. Previously we calculated the risk-neutral probability $q = 5/9 = 0.556$. The discount factor for the share is calculated using Equation (5.6) with $V_{up} = 125, V_{down} = 80$:

$$D_S = 0.897$$

corresponding to an expected return of 11.5%.

The discount factor for the call option with strike 102.5 is calculated using Equation (5.6) with $V_{up} = 22.5, V_{down} = 0$:

$$D_S = 0.756$$

corresponding to an expected return of 32.3%. Note that the share and the call option have different discount factors. The expected return on the call option is greater than that of the share, reflecting the greater risk of the call option. This should not be a surprise because we have already shown that the call is equivalent to a geared position in the stock.

Expectation pricing may be conceptually more appealing than risk-neutral pricing, but it involves unnecessary computation. For each derivative a specific discount factor must be calculated, depending on its risk (unlike risk-neutral pricing where we use the same risk-free discount rate for all derivatives). In fact, it turns out there is another way of writing the pricing equation that also allows us to work with real-world probabilities, but allows us to price all assets (including derivatives) using one set of discount factors. Let us examine this approach in the next section.

5.3.4. State prices and deflators

Of all the possible payoffs which might be analysed using the binomial tree, two deserve special attention. These are the two *Arrow-Debreu* securities (or state-price securities). These hypothetical assets pay one unit of currency in a particular future state of the world and zero otherwise. In the binomial example there are two such assets:

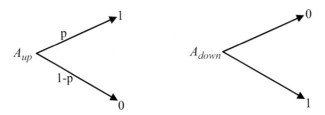

The prices of the Arrow-Debreu securities, A_{up} and A_{down}, are called state prices. Given these prices, we can calculate the appropriate discount factors of these securities. Using Equation (5.5) we have:

$$A_{up} = D_{up}p$$
$$A_{down} = D_{down}(1 - p)$$

These discount factors are called state-price deflators (or simply deflators).[8] The deflator corresponding to any particular state is the state price divided by the probability of that state. Using Equation (5.6),

$$D_{up} = \frac{q}{p} \times \frac{1}{1 + r}$$

$$D_{down} = \frac{1 - q}{1 - p} \times \frac{1}{1 + r}$$

(5.7)

So the deflators can be calculated by taking the ratio of the risk-neutral probabilities to the real-world probabilities and discounting at the risk-free rate.

Once we have calculated the two state prices, or equivalently the two deflators, they can be used to price any asset. Instead of replicating our general derivative using a portfolio of stocks and cash, we form a replicating

---

[8]The deflators is sometimes referred to as the 'state price density' or 'pricing kernel'.

portfolio consisting of *Arrow-Debreu* securities. The appropriate portfolio can be written down immediately – V_{up} units of the 'up security' and V_{down} of the 'down security.' So the current price of the derivative is:

$$V = V_{up}A_{up} + V_{down}A_{down}$$
$$= pD_{up}V_{up} + (1-p)D_{down}V_{down} \tag{5.8}$$

Written in this form, all assets (i.e., the 'fundamental' assets S and B, and all derivatives of these) can be priced by discounting using the same stochastic discount factors D_{up} and D_{down}, and taking the expectation using the real-world probability p.

Example:

Given our previous example $p = 0.7, q = 5/9$ the deflators are:

$$D_{up} = 0.756$$
$$D_{down} = 1.411$$

and hence the current value of the call option is:

$$C = 0.7 \times 0.756 \times 22.5 + 0.3 \times 1.411 \times 0 = 11.90$$

as we found using the risk-neutral approach.

Note that there is nothing special about the use of the 'real world' probabilities here. In general we can use any set of probabilities that we like and calculate a set of deflators using Equation (5.7). For example, we could work in a world in a which investors demand a greater expected return than we assume in the real-world (e.g. $p = 0.9$, implying an expected return on the stock of 20.5%) or even a world in which investors require a lower expected return than cash (e.g. $p = 0.5$, implying an expected return on the stock of 2.5%). Given our assumed probability, we can calculate a corresponding set of deflators, and all of these give rise to the same option prices.

Example:

Suppose that $p = 0.5$. The deflators corresponding to this choice of probability are:

$$D_{up} = 1.058$$
$$D_{down} = 0.847$$

Hence the current value of the call option is:

$$C = 0.5 \times 1.058 \times 22.5 + 0.5 \times 0.846 \times 0 = 11.90$$

as before.

Given that all choices of probability give rise to the same price, the choice of which probability to use is often motivated by the ease of calculation. In practice it is often simplest to use risk-neutral probabilities ($p = q$) in which case the deflators are simply the cash discount factors.

5.3.5. *Beyond the single-step binomial tree*

5.3.5.1. *Two-step binomial trees*

The one-step binomial example may appear unrealistically simple, but it illustrates some very general principles that continue to hold for more complex (and realistic) models. As a first attempt to generalise the model, let us consider extending the model to two binomial steps. As in the single-step example, we analyse a risky asset that can rise by 25% (with real world probability $p = 0.7$), or fall by 20% each year. The two-step tree for the share price is then:[9]

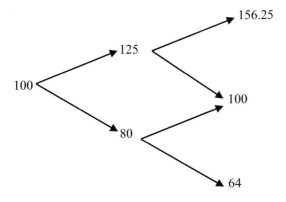

---

[9]Note that the model is constructed in such a way that the tree is recombining i.e., an up-move followed by a down-move gives the same share price as a down-move followed by an up-move.

Suppose that we are offered a call option giving the owner the right to buy the share at a strike price $K = 90$ after 2 years. This option has the following tree:

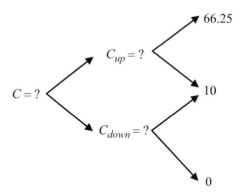

To calculate C, the price of the option today, we use a technique called backwards induction. This involves starting at maturity and inductively working backwards through the tree, calculating the option values at each stage until we eventually reach the initial node. At maturity we know the value of the option. As explained in our discussion of the one-step example, the option is only exercised if the stock price exceeds the strike price (90), in which case the value is the difference between the stock price and the strike price. These values are shown on the tree drawn above. We then move back one time-step and calculate the option prices there. We can calculate the two possible option values, C_{up} and C_{down}, by considering the two one-step trees:

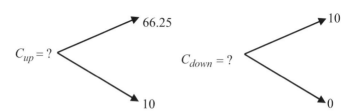

We already know the procedure for calculating C_{up} and C_{down}. We simply calculate the risk-neutral probabilities of each state occurring, calculate the expected value of the option under these probabilities, and discount at the risk-free rate. We already calculated the risk-neutral probability in the one-step example, $q = 5/9$, and hence:

$$C_{\text{up}} = \frac{1}{1.05} \times \left[\frac{5}{9} \times 66.25 + \frac{4}{9} \times 10\right] = 39.286$$

$$C_{\text{down}} = \frac{1}{1.05} \times \left[\frac{5}{9} \times 10 + \frac{4}{9} \times 0\right] = 5.291$$

We now move back another time-step, giving the following one-step tree:

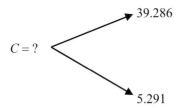

and once more use the risk-neutral pricing technique:

$$C = \frac{1}{1.05} \times \left[\frac{5}{9} \times 39.286 + \frac{4}{9} \times 5.291\right] = 23.03$$

Though we have performed this calculation in two stages, we could have arrived at the price in a single calculation. Note that we can write:

$$C = \frac{1}{1.05} \times \frac{1}{1.05} \times \left[\frac{5}{9} \times \frac{5}{9} \times 66.25 + 2 \times \frac{5}{9} \times \frac{4}{9} \times 10 + \frac{4}{9} \times \frac{4}{9} \times 0\right]$$

$$= \frac{1}{(1+r)^2} \times \left[q^2 C_{\text{up,up}} + 2q(1-q)C_{\text{up,down}} + (1-q)^2 C_{\text{down,down}}\right]$$

$$(5.9)$$

where $C_{\text{up,up}}$ is the value of the option after two up-steps, etc. Compare this to Equation (5.3) for the one-step tree. In both cases we calculate the expected option payoff in all states (using the risk-neutral probabilities of each of these states occurring) and discount using the risk-free interest rate.

In addition to the fair value of the option, we can also calculate the replicating portfolio i.e., the unique portfolio of underlying stock and cash which replicates the payoff of the option in all 3 states of the world. As we consider multiple time-steps, the nature of the replicating portfolio changes dynamically at each step.

As outlined in Section 5.3.3.2 above, the number of units of stock which we should hold at any point is $\Delta = (V_{up} - V_{down})/S_{up} - S_{down}$. In option pricing terminology, this is called the 'delta' of the option. In the current example, the delta changes as follows:

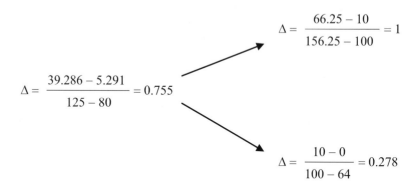

$$\Delta = \frac{39.286 - 5.291}{125 - 80} = 0.755$$

$$\Delta = \frac{66.25 - 10}{156.25 - 100} = 1$$

$$\Delta = \frac{10 - 0}{100 - 64} = 0.278$$

Note that, if the stock price increases over the first time-step, the delta becomes 1. In this state of the world, the option is guaranteed to expire in-the-money i.e., the call option will definitely be exercised and hence we need to hold exactly one unit of stock.

As in the one-step tree we can re-write this equation more generally in terms of a specified set of probabilities and their associated deflators. Since there are 3 possible states after two time-steps there are three Arrow-Debreu securities $A_{up,up}, A_{up,down}$ and $A_{down,down}$, and hence 3 deflators $D_{up,up}, D_{up,down}$ and $D_{down,down}$. These are defined as before: the Arrow-Debreu securities are assets paying 1 unit of currency in each state of the world and the deflator is the corresponding discount factor, obtained by dividing the state price by the (real-world) probability of that state:

$$A_{up,up} = D_{up,up}p^2$$

$$A_{up,down} = D_{up,down}p(1-p)$$

$$A_{down,down} = D_{down,down}(1-p)^2$$

By calculating the state-prices using risk-neutral pricing we find:

$$D_{up,up} = \frac{1}{(1+r)^2} \times \frac{q^2}{p^2}$$

$$D_{up,down} = \frac{1}{(1+r)^2} \times \frac{q(1-q)}{p(1-p)}$$

$$D_{\text{down,down}} = \frac{1}{(1+r)^2} \times \frac{(1-q)^2}{(1-p)^2}$$

Hence we can re-write Equation (5.9) as:

$$C = p^2 D_{\text{up,up}} C_{\text{up,up}} + 2p(1-p) D_{\text{up,down}} C_{\text{up,down}}$$
$$+ (1-p)^2 D_{\text{down,down}} C_{\text{down,down}}$$

5.3.5.2. Multi-step trees

The techniques described above generalise to any number of time-steps. In general the value of a derivative in an n-step model can be written:

$$V = \frac{1}{(1+r)^n} E_Q[V_n] \tag{5.10}$$

where V_n is the value of the derivative after n time-steps and $E_Q[\cdots]$ denotes taking the expectation using the risk-neutral probability q. This is the risk-neutral pricing equation.

In particular we can calculate the prices of the *Arrow-Debreu* securities. The price of a security paying £1 in state i is:

$$A_n(\text{state\_}i) = \frac{1}{(1+r)^n} \text{Pr}_Q[\text{state\_}i] \tag{5.11}$$

where $\text{Pr}_Q[\text{state\_}i]$ denotes the probability of state i using the risk-neutral probability q. The corresponding deflators are defined by dividing by the real-world state probability:

$$D_n(\text{state\_}i) = \frac{A_n(\text{state\_}i)}{\text{Pr}_P[\text{state\_}i]}$$

where $\text{Pr}_P[\text{state\_}i]$ denotes the probability of state i using the real-world probability p. Using Equation (5.11), the deflators can be expressed in terms of the ratio of the risk-neutral probability to the real-world probability:

$$D_n(\text{state\_}i) = \frac{1}{(1+r)^n} \times \frac{\text{Pr}_Q[\text{state\_}i]}{\text{Pr}_P[\text{state\_}i]} \tag{5.12}$$

We can use deflators to price any derivative:

$$V = E_P[D_n V_n] \tag{5.13}$$

5.4. Conclusions

A once-in-a-lifetime change to actuarial valuation practice is about to take place with the adoption of market-consistent valuation methods. We believe that this is good news. However, the implementation of the new thinking presents some significant challenges for actuaries, accountants and pension practitioners. In this chapter we have presented a simple example to give the reader some intuition for the ideas behind market-consistent, fair values. In addition, we have explained the basic ideas behind valuation of contingent claims using both the risk-neutral pricing techniques and the equivalent 'state price deflator' approach.

Fair Value and Pension Fund Management
N. Kortleve, T. Nijman and E. Ponds (Editors)

CHAPTER 6

Valuation and Risk Management of Inflation-Sensitive Pension Rights

Theo E. Nijman[a] and Ralph S.J. Koijen[b]
(Tilburg University)

Abstract

The introduction of the new international accounting standard requires that assets and liabilities are valued at market value. Since pension liabilities are generally to some extent indexed according to inflation, this provides new challenges for both valuation and risk management. This chapter discusses models that can be used to determine the fair value of inflation-sensitive pension rights. In addition, we show how these models can be used in risk management applications and we emphasize the discrepancy between currently popular methodologies, like duration analysis. We show that in case of pension schemes where indexation is conditional on the state of the pension fund, the value of the liabilities is determined by an interplay between economic variables, like interest rates and inflation, and the asset mix. A thorough understanding of such dependencies is crucial in order to come to a proper assessment of the risks to which the liabilities are exposed.

Keywords: inflation-sensitive liabilities, pricing kernel, valuation

JEL codes: E31, G13, G23

6.1. Introduction

Pension rights can easily be eroded by inflation. For this reason, many pension schemes offer indexation of retirement benefits to annual changes in a

[a]Department of Finance, Tilburg University, PO Box 90153, 5000 LE Tilburg, the Netherlands, E-mail: Nijman@TilburgUniversity.nl; [b]Department of Finance, Tilburg University, PO Box 90153, 5000 LE Tilburg, the Netherlands, E-mail: R.S.J.Koijen@TilburgUniversity.nl

consumer price index (CPI). Retirees are therefore insulated from inflation risk, at least as long as their preferred consumption bundle is not too different from the consumption bundle used to compute the CPI. Some pension schemes also aim at indexation to the overall welfare level and index with respect to wage rather than price inflation. Full (price-)indexation is offered by real annuities as they are widely available in the UK and of which examples can be found in other markets as well (see e.g. Brown *et al.* (2001)). Full indexation has also been offered for many years by the US social security system as well as by many defined benefit schemes worldwide (e.g. in the US and in the Netherlands). Besides financial products and pension schemes that offer full indexation, recently products and pension schemes have also been designed that offer indexation to inflation in certain scenarios only, e.g. if the funding ratio of the defined benefit system is sufficiently high. Such schemes will be referred to in the sequel as conditionally indexed pension schemes.

Nominal pension rights are relatively easy to value using data on the market for nominal bonds. Assuming that longevity risk can be diversified, the market risk to which the nominal pension rights are exposed are the same as the risks in a corresponding portfolio of nominal bonds. Apart from the fact that the maturity structure will probably have to be somewhat extrapolated, the market price of such pension rights is easy to construct. Valuation of inflation-sensitive pension rights however is non-trivially harder than valuation of nominal pension rights, unless a sufficiently deep and liquid market for bonds indexed to the appropriate price index is available. Bonds that are indexed to price inflation are traded in many countries such as the UK, Sweden, Israel and nowadays also in France and the US (see Deacon *et al.* (2004) for an extensive overview). However, traded bonds are available for a limited number of maturities only, no bonds related to wage inflation or local price inflation within e.g. the US are available, and the markets do not even exist for many other countries or are highly illiquid (including e.g. Germany and the Netherlands). Clearly also the value of the conditional indexation schemes that were referred to cannot be derived directly from market prices of traded assets. In this chapter we discuss how pricing models can be used to value inflation-sensitive pension rights, even if no perfectly equivalent assets are traded in the market.

Valuation of pension rights is important for many reasons. First of all, market valuation of the pension rights increases the transparency of a pension scheme and helps the beneficiary to choose between alternatives, such as nominal or real annuities and/or voluntary participation in a collective pension scheme. Valuation of the pension rights is also required to compute a fair premium for new entrants to be included in a pension scheme as well as for transfers out of the scheme. Supervisory authorities will need the value of the liabilities of a pension fund in order to be able to judge its solvency. Adequate risk management of that fund (e.g. to protect indexation rights) moreover requires that one realizes how the value of assets and liabilities will fluctuate if underlying fundamentals fluctuate, which requires once more valuation. Moreover, valuation of the liabilities can be a powerful tool in labour agreement negotiations to confront parties with the monetary value of elements of the pension deal, and is required to determine generational accounts, which illustrates solidarity issues within the pension scheme, see also Kortleve and Ponds (2006) and Exley (2006). Finally, valuation of inflation-sensitive assets is of course also relevant for topics far from the applications to pensions and retirement on which we focus, e.g. in valuing an inflation-sensitive firm.

The plan of this chapter is as follows. In Section 6.2, we discuss how valuation of pension liabilities and models of the term structure are related. In Section 6.3, we will first sketch an overly simple term structure model along the lines of duration analysis that can be used to value nominal or fully indexed liabilities, assuming that certain strong additional assumptions have been satisfied. This model, which is often used in risk management for 'back of the envelope' calculations, is shown to be severely misspecified. In Section 6.4, we introduce the use of models of the real and nominal term structure to value inflation-sensitive assets. In line with the recent literature (Evans (1998); Campbell and Viceira (2001); Brennan and Xia (2002); Ang and Bekaert (2004)) we discuss how pricing kernels can be specified which can be used to price nominal, real as well as conditionally indexed liabilities. Moreover, we will indicate briefly how valuation along these lines is related to pricing through a replicating strategy, to risk neutral valuation, and to state contingent discounting, see also Hibbert *et al.* (2006). Section 6.5 will present a number of numerical results, where we focus on valuation of the conditional indexation contracts that have been implemented in the Netherlands as of the year 2004. In Section 6.6, the same numerical example is used in order to illustrate the use of models for the purpose of risk management. Section 6.7 concludes and provides references to recent literature to extend the models to be more aligned with observed market data. Moreover, we will discuss several practical limitations of the approach.

6.2. Valuation of nominal and real pension rights

Valuation of straight real (nominal) pension rights requires knowledge of the real (nominal) term structure. In order to be able to discuss term structure models and to link them to valuation, we will first introduce some notation. A nominal discount bond maturing in period $t + n$ is a bond that pays the principal (normalized at 1) in period $t + n$ and never pays any coupon. The price of such a nominal bond in period t will be denoted as $P_t^{(n)}$. The yield to maturity (i.e., the nominal interest rate) of a discount bond is defined as $R_t^{(n)}$ that solves

$$P_t^{(n)} = \left(1 + R_t^{(n)}\right)^{-n} \tag{6.1}$$

Since $\log(1 + x) \approx x$ for x close to zero this definition is approximately equivalent to

$$P_t^{(n)} = e^{-nR_t^{(n)}} \tag{6.2}$$

In the sequel, we will use Equation (6.2) for mathematical convenience.

The set of interest rates a $(R_t^{(n)})$ at a specific point in time (t) with varying maturities (n) is known as the nominal term structure of interest rates. Likewise, a real or indexed bond is a bond that pays one real unit at maturity. If the underlying price index is denoted as Π_t, the pay-off at maturity will be Π_{t+n}/Π_t in nominal terms. The pay-off of a real bond is therefore scaled proportionally to the increase in the price index. Fully analogous to the nominal case, the yield to maturity (i.e., the real interest rate) of a real discount bond is defined as $R_t^{R(n)}$ that solves

$$P_t^{R(n)} = e^{-nR_t^{R(n)}} \tag{6.3}$$

Now consider the market value of a pension scheme that generates cash flow F_{t+n} in period $t + n$. These cash flows are in principle random variables, and might depend e.g. on future inflation, on survival of the participants etc. By definition of the expected return $\mu_t^{(n)}$, the market value at time t of the cash flow at time $t + n, V_t^{(n)}$, can be written as

$$V_t^{(n)} = \mathbb{E}_t\left(F_{t+n}e^{-n\mu_t^{(n)}}\right) \tag{6.4}$$

where $\mathbb{E}_t$ denotes the conditional expectation operator, where the conditioning takes place on all information available at time t. Consequently, the value of the pension scheme can be written as

$$V_t = \sum_{n=1}^{N} V_t^{(n)} = \sum_{n=1}^{N} \mathbb{E}_t\left(F_{t+n}e^{-n\mu_t^{(n)}}\right) \tag{6.5}$$

Equations (6.4) and (6.5) are not very informative, unless the expected returns, $\mu_t^{(n)}$, are known. This is the case if the cash flows are non-random, but also, for example, if micro-longevity risk is the only source of randomness.[1] We assume throughout that the size of the pension fund is sufficiently large to diversify longevity risk. Since all randomness in the cash flow is fully diversifiable, standard finance theory imposes that it will not be priced, i.e., the expected return equals the corresponding nominal interest rate, implying that

$$V_t = \sum_{n=1}^{N} \mathbb{E}_t\left(F_{t+n}e^{-nR_t^{(n)}}\right) = \sum_{n=1}^{N} P_t^{(n)}\mathbb{E}_t(F_{t+n}) \tag{6.6}$$

Valuation of indexed pension schemes is possible using the real term structure along the same lines. First, denote the one period inflation rate corresponding to the relevant price index Π_t as

$$\pi_{t+1} = \log \Pi_{t+1} - \log \Pi_t \tag{6.7}$$

and define average inflation over n periods as

$$\pi_{t+n}^{(n)} = \frac{1}{n}\sum_{i=1}^{n} \pi_{t+i} = \frac{1}{n}(\log \Pi_{t+1} - \log \Pi_t)$$

We denote the risk premium that alters the nominal interest rate in order to account for inflation risk by $\lambda_t^{(n)}$. Using this notation, the market value of

---

[1] Micro-longevity risk is caused by the randomness of deaths for given survival probabilities. Macro-longevity risk, which is due to changes in the survival probabilities due to e.g. improvements in health care, is beyond the scope of this chapter.

the indexed pension scheme can be written as

$$
V_t^R = \sum_{n=1}^{N} \mathbb{E}_t \left(\frac{\Pi_{t+n}}{\Pi_t} F_{t+n} e^{-n\left(R_t^{(n)} + \lambda_t^{(n)}\right)} \right)
$$

$$
= \sum_{n=1}^{N} \mathbb{E}_t \left(F_{t+n} e^{-n\left(R_t^{(n)} + \lambda_t^{(n)} - \pi_{t+n}^{(n)}\right)} \right)
$$

$$
\approx \sum_{n=1}^{N} \mathbb{E}_t \left(F_{t+n} e^{-n\left(R_t^{R(n)}\right)} \right) = \sum_{n=1}^{N} P_t^{R(n)} \mathbb{E}_t (F_{t+n})
$$

(6.8)

where we define the real interest rate of an n period bond as

$$
R_t^{R(n)} = R_t^{(n)} - \mathbb{E}_t \left(\pi_{t+n}^{(n)} \right) + \lambda_t^{(n)}
$$

(6.9)

Many models assume that inflation risk is not priced, i.e., the expected return on nominal bonds coincides with that on indexed bonds, in which case $\lambda_t^{(n)}$ vanishes. If the assumption is valid, the real term structure can be obtained through knowledge of the nominal term structure and inflation expectations only.

If the relevant term structure (either the nominal or the real) is observed for every maturity, term structure models are not required to value the pension scheme if the pension scheme is either fully nominal or real. For most developed countries, data on the nominal term structure are readily accessible, but typically only for maturities up to a limited number of years. In many countries, the swap curve generates yields for maturities, approximately, up to fifty years. Valuation of pension schemes requires assumptions on the interest rate for even longer maturities, which can be obtained through modelling. More importantly, term structure data for indexed bonds are available for a limited number of countries, for specific choices of the index used for indexation (e.g. price rather than wage inflation), and for very particular maturities only. Term structure models can be used to estimate interest rates that are not directly observed. As a consequence, the valuation of either nominal or real pension schemes will typically rely on the specification of the model that also implies a specific term structure.

Modelling is even more crucial if no assets are traded that are closely related to the liabilities to be valued. This represents the current case of pension funds in countries where no inflation-linked products are traded, or markets are highly illiquid. In Section 6.5, we will consider the example of conditional indexation schemes as they have been recently introduced in the Netherlands. Given this particular pension scheme, we will show that the value of the liabilities is dependent on the asset mix, the current state of the economy, and the current state of the pension fund.

6.3. Risk management of nominal and real pension rights using duration analysis

As discussed in Section 6.2, term structure models and assumptions regarding parameters such as the inflation risk premium are sometimes required for valuation of nominal or real pension rights, when no indexed securities are traded within the economy. Even if the relevant term structure is fully observed, i.e., no modelling assumptions are required for valuation, the models are essential for risk managing and risk budgeting of trustees and participants of pension schemes. Through the use of pricing models 'what if' questions can be answered, which give the value of the scheme if the interest rate drops, the inflation rate rises etc. and which enable portfolio strategies that would hedge the surplus of the fund. Duration analysis is currently one of the most popular tools for this aim.

Duration analysis is based on assumptions on the sensitivity of the market value of assets with respect to fluctuations in the interest rates. Duration analysis assumes that the fluctuations in interest rates with arbitrary maturities can be adequately described by fluctuations in one rate (say the short rate) only. The relative interest rate exposure of a nominal zero coupon bond with arbitrary maturity n with respect to the short rate can be written as

$$\varepsilon = \frac{1}{P_t^{(n)}} \frac{\partial P_t^{(n)}}{\partial R_t^{(1)}} = -n \frac{\partial R_t^{(n)}}{\partial R_t^{(1)}} \tag{6.10}$$

where the second equality follows from Equation (6.2).

According to duration analysis, a 1% increase in the short rate implies a 1% increase in the interest rates with all other maturities, i.e., duration analysis allows for parallel shift in the term structure only. This is illustrated in Figure 6.1.

**Figure 6.1.   Impact of changes in the interest rate on the term structure
if the assumptions underlying duration analysis are satisfied. Only shifts
in a parallel fashion can occur according to duration analysis**

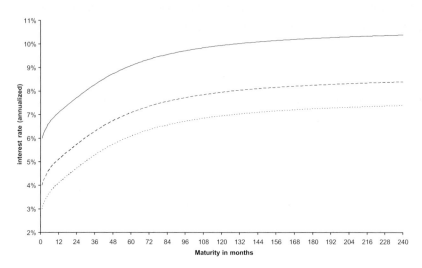

This assumption implies that the interest exposure of a zero coupon bond
duration n (i.e., with n periods to maturity) simplifies to

$$\varepsilon = -n \tag{6.11}$$

Equation (6.11) states the important result that, within the assumptions made,
the interest exposure of a zero coupon bond happens to coincide with the
duration of the bond. This explains the terminology 'duration analysis'.

In an analogous way the relative interest rate exposure of a portfolio as
in Equation (6.6) can be obtained as

$$\varepsilon_V = \frac{1}{V_t}\frac{\partial V_t}{\partial R_t^{(1)}} = -\frac{\sum_{n=1}^{N} nV_t^{(n)}}{V_t}\frac{\partial R_t^{(n)}}{\partial R_t^{(1)}} \tag{6.12}$$

which simplifies under the assumptions of duration analysis to

$$\varepsilon_V = -\frac{\sum_{n=1}^{N} nV_t^{(n)}}{V_t} \tag{6.13}$$

i.e., the duration of the portfolio is simply the weighted duration of each of
the assets or liabilities. The duration of the liabilities of a pension scheme is

often in the range 15–20 years. According to duration analysis this implies that the market value of the liabilities will rise by 15–20% if the interest rate drops 1%. For a more detailed textbook treatment of duration analysis and the use of convexity corrections to obtain second order approximations to the sensitivity of market values to interest rate changes, see for instance Campbell *et al.* (1997) and Jarrow and Turnbull (2000).

The argument underlying duration analysis can be extended in a straight-forward way to the analysis of real rather than nominal bonds by referring to real rather than nominal interest rates. Both the nominal and the real term structure will shift in parallel fashion if, on top of the assumptions on the nominal curve, shifts in the inflation risk premium $\lambda_t^{(n)}$ and the expected average annual inflation $\mathbb{E}_t\left(\pi_{t+n}^{(n)}\right)$ are identical for all maturities.

Duration analysis is heavily used in applications and is an important tool for 'back of the envelope' calculations. It should be realized however that the model underlying duration analysis is severely misspecified for at least two reasons

1. The model allows for parallel shifts in the term structure only;
2. The model implies that long rates are as volatile as short rates.

Both assumptions are in contrast with the stylized facts in the data, see e.g. Brandt and Chapman (2002). In the next section we will introduce a model that relaxes the assumption underlying duration analysis, i.e., $\partial R_t^{(n)}/\partial R_t^{(1)}$ is not necessarily equal to 1. This model illustrates that duration analysis based on the fluctuations of short rates overemphasizes the exposure to interest rate risk in the market value of pension schemes, due to the implicit assumption that long rates are as volatile as short rates.

6.4. The use of pricing kernels to value inflation-sensitive assets

In Section 6.2, we discussed how nominal or real pension schemes can be valued at market value using observations or assumptions on the nominal and real term structure, respectively. Valuation of more general inflation-sensitive assets and liabilities, such as the conditionally indexed pension schemes, as referred to in the introduction, requires additional modelling. In this section, we will introduce the notion of a pricing kernel and show how it can be used to derive term structure models and to price interest and inflation-sensitive assets. Moreover, we will explain how the model can be used for risk management and how the model avoids the limitations of duration analysis that were referred to in Section 6.3.

To motivate the nature of the pricing kernel, consider a two period economy, where an agent maximizes expected utility and the utility function of the agent (U) is time-separable, i.e., can be written as

$$\mathbb{E}_t(U(C_t, C_{t+1})) = u(C_t) + \varphi \mathbb{E}_t(u(C_{t+1}))$$

where C_t denotes consumption at time t and u the utility index of the investor. The parameter φ is the subjective discount factor which captures the impatience of the agent, i.e., consumption today is preferred over consumption next period ($\varphi \in (0, 1)$). The income that the agent receives from an exogenous source, say labour income, will be denoted L_t. Next period's income, L_{t+1}, is a random variable. Now assume that a number of financial assets is traded in this economy with corresponding price vector P_t at time t. Next period's price vector, P_{t+1}, is a vector of random variables. The agent has to decide on his portfolio choice, i.e., will have to choose the number of units of each of the financial assets that will be held, which is reflected in the vector θ. Formally, the agent solves the problem[2]

$$\max_{\theta} u(C_t) + \varphi \mathbb{E}_t(u(C_{t+1}))$$

$$s.t. \ C_t = L_t - \theta^\mathsf{T} P_t, C_{t+1} = L_{t+1} + \theta^\mathsf{T} P_{t+1}$$

Substituting the constraints into the objective and setting the derivative with respect to θ equal to zero yields the first order condition for an optimal consumption and portfolio choice[3]

$$P_t = \mathbb{E}_t(M_{t+1} P_{t+1}) \qquad\qquad (6.14)$$

where

$$M_{t+1} = \varphi \frac{u_c(C_{t+1})}{u_c(C_t)} \qquad\qquad (6.15)$$

where u_c represents the marginal utility of consumption.

---

[2] In this illustration we do not consider portfolio constraints like short-sale constraints or borrowing constraints.

[3] Conditions on the utility function ensure that the necessary first order condition is sufficient for the optimal portfolio allocation.

Because of Equation (6.15), the pricing kernel is often referred to as the marginal rate of substitution. It is also known as the stochastic discount factor, since M_{t+1} discounts future pay-offs to their current value. Assuming that satiation does not occur, M_{t+1} is positive since the marginal utility of consumption will be positive. In general, when arbitrage opportunities are excluded in financial markets, the existence of a positive pricing kernel is ensured.

Although Equation (6.14) has here been derived for simplicity in a two period economy it can be shown that the relation is equally valid in a multi-period setting. Moreover, it can be shown that the assumption that the agent maximizes an expected time separable utility function is not needed to obtain Equation (6.14); direct use of the law of one price and exclusion of arbitrage opportunities yields the same result (see e.g. Cochrane (2001)).

The pricing kernel is a very powerful tool for valuation of all assets for which the joint distribution of the kernel and the future pay-off of the asset has to be modelled. Many influential papers in the recent literature on modelling nominal and real interest rates rely on specifications of the pricing kernel (see e.g. Campbell and Viceira (2001); Brennan and Xia (2002); Ang and Piazzesi (2003) and Ang and Bekaert (2004)). The use of the pricing kernel is probably best explained by considering a specific example. Assume that the prices of nominal and real bonds of all maturities as well as the stock market index in a specific economy are determined by a single state vector only. This state vector, x_t, could consist e.g. of the nominal annual interest rate, the annual inflation rate, and the return on the stock market index. Assume that the state vector is generated by a first order vector autoregressive process

$$x_{t+1} = \mu + \Gamma(x_t - \mu) + \varepsilon_{t+1} \qquad (6.16)$$

where $\varepsilon_{t+1} \overset{i.i.d.}{\sim} N(0, \Sigma)$. Assume in addition that the logarithm of the pricing kernel can be written as

$$- \log M_{t+1} = \alpha + \delta^\mathsf{T} x_t + \beta^\mathsf{T} \varepsilon_{t+1} + \eta_{t+1} \qquad (6.17)$$

where $\eta_{t+1} \overset{i.i.d.}{\sim} N(0, \sigma_\eta^2)$ and ε_s and η_t are mutually independent for all t and s. See Campbell *et al.* (1997) for a motivation of this pricing kernel specification. Given this representation of the pricing kernel, modelling is tantamount to specification of the prices of risk, β.

Equation (6.14) can be used to price all assets that do not depend on η_{t+1}, the unspecified component of the pricing kernel. The reason is that σ_n^2 is not identified on the basis of the assets traded, since the innovations in the traded assets are solely determined by ε_{t+1}, which is by construction orthogonal to η_{t+1}.

To price the assets, one way is to compute the expectation in Equation (6.14) through Monte Carlo simulation of Equations (6.16) and (6.17). Consider an asset with a single pay-off at time $t + n$, e.g. a European option that matures at time $t + n$. Let the function $P_{t+n}(x_{t+1}, \ldots, x_{t+n})$ denote how the pay-off depends on the future states of the economy. Substitution of (6.14) in itself and applying the law of iterated expectations yields

$$P_t = \mathbb{E}_t\left(P_{t+n}(x_{t+1}, \ldots, x_{t+n}) \prod_{i=1}^{n} M_{t+i}\right) \qquad (6.18)$$

The asset can be priced by approximating the expectation in Equation (6.18) through Monte Carlo simulation of the state vector as well as the kernel simultaneously. Let $x_{t+s}^{(k)}$ and $M_{t+s}^{(k)}$ denote simulation result for period $t + s$ ($s = 1, \ldots, n$) in replication k ($k = 1, \ldots, K$). As K tends to infinity, the empirical mean

$$\hat{P}_t = \frac{1}{K} \sum_{k=1}^{K} \left[P_{t+n}\left(x_{t+1}^{(k)}, \ldots, x_{t+n}^{(k)} \prod_{i=1}^{n} M_{t+i}^{(k)}\right) \right] \qquad (6.19)$$

will converge in probability to the true price of the asset on the basis of the weak law of large numbers. In order to limit the computational effort, it may turn out to be useful to employ variance reduction techniques in order to reduce the sampling error. Examples are importance sampling, antithetic variables and control variates, see for instance Glasserman (2003). Along the same lines, the value of a portfolio with cash flows at several points in time can be determined by adding the value of each of the components.

Monte Carlo simulation will be in used in Section 6.5 to value inflation-sensitive liabilities of a particular pension scheme. The model structure that is chosen is such that analytical expressions can be obtained for the price of nominal as well as real bonds. It is well known (see for instance Campbell *et al.* (1997); Campbell and Viceira (2001)) that the specific model structure in Equations (6.16) and (6.17) implies, if the prices of risk, β, are affine in the state variables, for the nominal term structure of interest rates

$$\log P_t^{(n)} = -na_{x,n} - nb_{x,n}^{\mathsf{T}} x_t \tag{6.20}$$

and for the real term structure of interest rates

$$\log P_t^{R(n)} = -na_{x,n}^R - nb_{x,n}^{R\mathsf{T}} x_t \tag{6.21}$$

where the coefficients $a_{x,n}$, $b_{x,n}$, $a_{x,n}^R$ and $b_{x,n}^R$ are known functions of the parameters in Equations (6.16) and (6.17). The model in Equations (6.20) and (6.21) is typically referred to as an affine term structure model, because Equations (6.2) and (6.3) imply that the nominal and real term yields are affine in the state vector. The appendix provides more details on the derivation of Equations (6.20) and (6.21) and specifies explicitly how the coefficients in these equations can be determined from those in Equations (6.16) and (6.17).

Note that Equations (6.20) and (6.21) can also be used as tool for hedging and risk management in order to generalize duration analysis. Equations (6.20) and (6.21) describe how the value of nominal and real bonds with various maturities will depend on the vector of state variables. In duration analysis, only one state variable is considered (the level of the term structure) and the interest exposure of all bonds is set equal to the duration, n, of the bond (i.e., $b_{x,n} = 1$ is imposed for all n). An application of use of Equations (6.20) and (6.21) in risk management will be discussed in Section 6.6.

As is well known in the option pricing literature, the use of pricing kernels to value assets is equivalent to several other approaches to valuation (see e.g. Cochrane (2001)). In case of complete markets, the use of the pricing kernel as outlined above is equivalent to pricing by replication. In case of incomplete markets, it is no longer possible to replicate any contingent claim and the pricing kernel is not uniquely defined. Consequently, infinitely many valid pricing kernels exist that price all traded assets correctly. Apart from modelling the asset dynamics, which is required both in complete and incomplete markets, this requires additional modelling of the pricing kernel. In this chapter, we have assumed a particular specification of the pricing kernel that is often used in finance theory. We assume that the prices of risk are constant, in line with e.g. Campbell and Viceira (2001). Alternatively, the prices of risk may be assumed to be affine in the factors, leading to essentially affine models that have been introduced by Duffee (2002) and applied in discrete time by Ang and Piazzesi (2003).

For the sake of completeness, we remark that the use of the pricing kernel is also equivalent to the use of state contingent discounting or risk neutral valuation, see Hibbert *et al.* (2006). A specific model to compute discount factors implies a specific pricing kernel. Explicit specification of this kernel might be preferable to ensure consistency of the model parameters, the discount factors, and the true state probabilities.

6.5. Numerical example of the valuation of inflation-sensitive liabilities

In this section, we illustrate the use of the model that was developed in Section 6.4 for the valuation of the liabilities of a stylized pension scheme. We distinguish between valuation at actuarial value and valuation at market value. In case of valuation at market values, i.e., fair-value valuation, we distinguish between nominal, fully indexed, and conditionally indexed schemes. The results will indicate that in case of fair-value valuation, the value of the liabilities can depend on the current level of state vector, such as interest and inflation rates, and, in case of the conditional indexation schemes, also on the funding ratio of the scheme and even on the asset mix. Throughout, we consider that the model structure that is used in valuation as given. Model-based valuation as proposed here clearly implies the risk that models or parameters are misspecified and leads to new questions related to adequate use of models and supervision. These issues will be discussed in Section 6.7.

The pension scheme that we consider in this example has linearly decreasing expected cash flows over the subsequent 60 years. The actuarial value of the liabilities (i.e., the value obtained by discounting all future cash flows at 4%) is set to 1000. The duration of the liabilities equals 13 years. These two assumptions fully determine the liability structure which is illustrated in Figure 6.2.

Note that we take a discontinuity perspective, i.e., we abstract from new premium inflows. Actuarial risks in the nominal cash flows are assumed to be fully diversifiable, which implies that this risk can be ignored for valuation purposes. In case of indexed or conditionally index pension schemes, the cash flows will obviously depend on future inflation.

The model that is used in valuation is a special case of the model introduced in Section 6.4. We assume for the dynamics of the state variables

$$R_{t+1}^{R(1)} = \mu_R + \varphi_R\left(R_t^{R(1)} - \mu_R\right) + \varepsilon_{t+1}^R \tag{6.22}$$

Figure 6.2.   Liabilities structure of the artificial pension fund considered in Section 6.5. Depending on the assumptions regarding indexation scheme that has been put in place, these cash flows are indexed annually. The linearly declining scheme implies that we do not consider new premium inflows

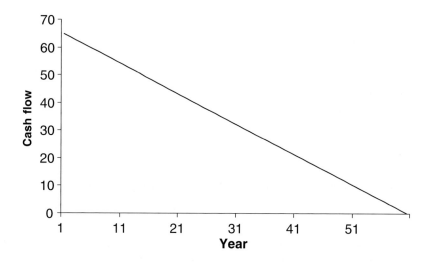

$$\pi_{t+1} = \mu_\pi + \varphi_\pi (\pi_t - \mu_\pi) + \varepsilon_{t+1}^\pi \tag{6.23}$$

$$r_{t+1} = \mu_r + R_t^{(1)} + \varepsilon_{t+1}^r \tag{6.24}$$

where R^R, π and r denote, respectively the real short rate, one period inflation and stock returns. For notational convenience, we define

$$\varepsilon_{t+1} = \left[\varepsilon_{t+1}^R \ \varepsilon_{t+1}^\pi \ \varepsilon_{t+1}^r \right]^{\mathrm{T}}$$

where $\varepsilon_{t+1} \overset{i.i.d.}{\sim} N(0_{3\times 1}, \Sigma)$. For the specification of the real pricing kernel[4] (M_{t+1}), we postulate

$$-\log M_{t+1} = R_t^{R(1)} + \alpha + \beta_R \varepsilon_{t+1}^R + \beta_r \varepsilon_{t+1}^r + \eta_{t+1} \tag{6.25}$$

---

[4]The relation between the nominal and real pricing kernel is given by $M_{t+1}^\$ (\Pi_{t+1}/\Pi_t) = M_{t+1}$ where $M_{t+1}^\$$ denotes the nominal pricing kernel and M_{t+1} indicates the real pricing kernel.

In principle, the parameters in Equations (6.22–6.25) can be estimated from observed data, as discussed in e.g. Ang and Piazzesi (2003), Campbell and Viceira (2001) and Brennan and Xia (2002). Commonly used estimation procedures are maximum likelihood and GMM. For this illustration, we did not estimate the parameters along these lines, but rather selected, in an admittedly somewhat ad hoc way, a set of parameters that reflects the main stylized facts in the data. The data show that inflation and interest changes are highly persistent, and that long rates are less volatile than short rates: The choice of the parameters is based on the assumption that the real interest rates and inflation move independently. If we in addition assume that stock returns are independent of inflation and the process for the real short rate, the implied covariance matrix of the innovations Σ has a diagonal structure. The diagonal elements are selected so that the standard deviation of the innovations in real rates, inflation rates and stock returns is 1.1%, 0.8% and 15.5%, respectively, which is roughly in line with historical data. Regarding the unconditional expectation of the state variables, we assumed that the unconditionally expected real rate (μ_R) is set to 4.0%, the corresponding figure for the inflation rate (μ_π) is 2.0%, while the equity risk premium (μ_r) is assumed to be 3.0%, which determines together with the stock return volatility β_r. The persistence parameters for the real rate and the inflation rate (φ_R and φ_π) are set to 0.94 and 0.90, respectively. The long-term bond risk premium, i.e., the premium for holding nominal bonds with fifty rather than one year to maturity, is set to 2%, which rejects the pure expectation hypothesis. This assumption determines β_R, which reflects the price of interest rate risk. Note that in Equation (6.25) we have already assumed that inflation risk is not priced, i.e., the expected return of nominal and real bonds with the same maturity differs only due to an exposition of Jensen's inequality. Formally, this is reflected into the fact that $\beta_\pi = 0$, which has been incorporated already into the above-mentioned pricing kernel specification. We assume in this example that all risk premia are constant, but the model can be extended to exhibit time-varying risk premia, without adding much complexity. From a practical perspective, it may be important to note that these models are generally not able to fit the initial term structure exactly. Models in the same spirit that do allow for an exact fit of the current term structure are proposed by Hull and White (1996).

It should be noted that when pensions are indexed against wage rather than price inflation, this can be incorporated as well. A convenient way to accomplish this is to model wage inflation as price inflation plus an additional innovation. This risk factor, which determines the discrepancy between price and wage inflation, can be priced in the pricing kernel which leads to a real term structure on the basis of wage rather than price inflation.

As indicated in Section 6.4, an important property of the model in Equations (6.22–6.25) is that it generates affine term structures. Rewriting Equations (6.20) and (6.21), we find

$$R_t^{(n)} = a_{y,n} + b_{y,n}^{\mathsf{T}} y_t \qquad (6.26)$$

for the nominal term structure, whereas for the real term structure, we obtain

$$R_t^{R(n)} = a_{y,n}^R + b_{y,n}^{R\mathsf{T}} y_t \qquad (6.27)$$

i.e., both the nominal and real term structure are affine in the state vector, which contains in this case $y_t = \left[R_t^{R(1)} \; \pi_t \; r_t^e \right]^{\mathsf{T}}$. We denote by r_t^e the return on stocks in excess of the nominal short rate. In Equations (6.22–6.24) we have chosen the state vector to reflect the real rate with one year to maturity and the current inflation rate. Using Equations (6.26) and (6.27), the selection of the state vector can be easily adjusted through rotation without affecting any of the results. Because the real rate is not directly observed in some countries, like e.g. the Netherlands, we will present several numerical results assuming that the nominal rate with one year to maturity and the current inflation rate constitute the state vector, which we denote by x_t once we add as a third element the excess return on stocks. The coefficients $a_{x,n}$, $b_{x,n}$, $a_{x,n}^R$ and $b_{x,n}^R$ with respect to the transformed state vector reflect the exposure of nominal and real rates with maturity n with respect to the annual nominal rate and current inflation. The coefficients are fully determined by the parameters in Equations (6.22–6.25), see the appendix.

The numerical values for the coefficients $a_{y,n}$, $b_{y,n}$, $a_{y,n}^R$ and $b_{y,n}^R$, as implied by the parameter assumptions referred to above are given in Table 6.1. Note that due to the independence of the process for the excess stock returns of the interest rate and inflation processes, excess stock returns do not have an impact on either the nominal or real term structure, i.e., $(b_{y,n})_3 = (b_{y,n}^R)_3 = 0$ for every n.

We provided the coefficients that correspond to the state vector y_t that contains the annual real rate and inflation, which are by assumption independent, to highlight the impact of changes in either of the factors. Note that long rates are much less sensitive to fluctuations in the annual real rate than short rates. Note also that inflation affects nominal rates positively, through

Table 6.1.   Implied coefficients of both the nominal and the real term structure of interest rates. In addition, the risk premium of holding an n period bond for one holding period is repeated in column 5

Maturity	$a_{y,n}$	$(b_{y,n})_1$	$(b_{y,n})_2$	Risk premium
1	0.20%	1.00	0.90	0.00%
2	0.52%	0.97	0.86	0.23%
3	0.83%	0.94	0.81	0.42%
4	1.11%	0.91	0.77	0.59%
5	1.38%	0.89	0.74	0.75%
10	2.49%	0.77	0.59	1.27%
20	4.00%	0.59	0.40	1.73%
30	4.93%	0.47	0.29	1.89%
50	5.98%	0.32	0.18	1.99%

Maturity	$a_{y,n}^R$	$\left(b_{y,n}^R\right)_1$	$\left(b_{y,n}^R\right)_2$	Risk premium
1	0.00%	1.00	0	0.00%
2	0.24%	0.97	0	0.24%
3	0.46%	0.94	0	0.44%
4	0.67%	0.91	0	0.63%
5	0.87%	0.89	0	0.80%
10	1.73%	0.77	0	1.40%
20	2.91%	0.59	0	1.96%
30	3.68%	0.47	0	2.17%
50	4.55%	0.32	0	2.29%

the assumption that the real rate and inflation are independent. In valuing nominal and real liabilities, we assume for simplicity that the model in Equations (6.22–6.25) perfectly fits the current nominal and real structure. In Section 6.6, we will see that, in case of market valuation, the exposure coefficients, $b_{y,n}$ and $b_{y,n}^R$, can play moreover a vital role in risk management of portfolios with interest and inflation-sensitive liabilities.

As a first illustration of the use of the model in Equations (6.22–6.25), we determine the fair value of nominal and fully indexed pension schemes and compare it to the actuarial value. In case of valuation at market value, the value of the scheme will depend on the current state vector, i.e., on the current nominal annual rate and inflation. We consider four cases for the current state of the economy, i.e., the nominal rate is either 5 or 7% and inflation equals either 2 or 4%. The nominal and real term structures implied by the model (and the parameter assumptions that have been made) are presented in Figures 6.3 and 6.4.

Figure 6.3.   Nominal and real term structures for different values of the initial state vector. The first element refers to the current nominal short rate, whereas the second element corresponds to the current 1 year inflation rate

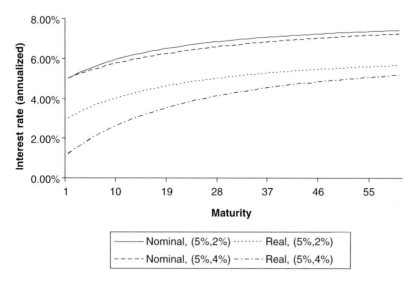

Figure 6.4.   Nominal and real term structures for different values of the initial state vector. The first element refers to the current nominal short rate, whereas the second element corresponds to the current 1 year inflation rate

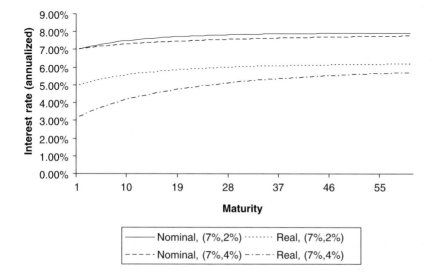

Table 6.2.   The nominal, real and actuarial value of the liabilities has been determined for different initial states of the economy. The nominal short rate equals either 5% or 7% , whereas the current inflation equals either 2% or 4%

Current 1 year nominal rate	Current inflation	Actuarial	Nominal	Real
5%	2%	1000	736.9	914.0
5%	4%	1000	755.2	1050.4
7%	2%	1000	644.1	788.3
7%	4%	1000	658.8	900.3

Using Equations (6.6) and (6.8) these term structures determine the market value of a nominal and real scheme.

Table 6.2 compares the impact of the selection of the discount factors on the value of the liabilities. The actuarial value obviously does not depend on the states and equals 1000 by construction. Figures 6.3 and 6.4 indicate that in all four cases the nominal term structure exceeds 4% for all maturities. It is therefore not surprising that the market value of a nominal pension with these expected cash flow is substantially less than 1000. As a first approximation to the value of these cash flows one could use duration analysis as discussed in Section 6.3. For example, the case where the nominal annual rate equals 7% and inflation 2%, the nominal term structure is approximately flat at the level of 7%. Duration analysis suggests that the value of the scheme is approximately 39% less than 1000 (i.e., from the actuarial 4% to the 'constant' 7%) since the duration of the liabilities is 13 years. As indicated before, the current model is somewhat more general than the one underlying duration analysis and not surprisingly the value obtained from the current model (644.1) does not fully coincide with the prediction of duration analysis (610).

The market value of fully indexed schemes is presented in the last column of Table 6.2. Discounting the expected nominal cash flows against the real rather than the nominal term structure implies that the market value of the liabilities increases substantially. The cost of indexation are estimated to be in the order of 20–40%, depending on the current state vector. The parameter assumptions made in this chapter imply that the market value of indexed liabilities is not too different from the actuarial value of the liabilities. Clearly, this is not the case though if the nominal interest rates are low and current inflation is high or the current nominal interest rate is high and the current inflation rate is low. Currently, funding ratios of pension funds are typically based on actuarial valuation of the liabilities. Comparison of the actuarial and market values of the liabilities is of course crucial to determine whether the use of market valuation will reduce the funding ratios further or will increase them.

Unlike valuation of the liabilities of straight nominal or indexed schemes as in Equations (6.6) and (6.8), consistent valuation of liabilities that include derivative components of some sort cannot easily be based on discounting expected future cash flows, since these discount rates are generally unknown. Equation (6.18) is equally valid for liabilities with derivative elements though and Monte Carlo analysis can be used for valuation using Equation (6.19), and therefore enables consistent valuation. Many types of derivative elements can occur in pension schemes. Some schemes offer stock market exposure but with a fixed minimum return. Many pension schemes in the UK are characterized by indexation up to a maximum inflation of, about 5%. In the Netherlands, many pension funds have introduced conditional indexation schemes of some form. These schemes offer only indexation if the funding ratio of the pension fund is sufficiently high. One example is a scheme that offers indexation if the nominal funding ratio is above 125% and none if this is not the case, see also Kortleve and Ponds (2006).

To illustrate valuation of liability schemes with conditional indexation and the value transfer that is implicit in a decision to switch from a fully indexed to a conditionally indexed scheme, we consider a specific conditional indexation scheme that roughly corresponds to the scheme adopted by ABP and PGGM. ABP and PGGM are by far the largest pension funds in the Netherlands and among the largest worldwide. ABP and PGGM have adopted a so-called policy ladder ('indexatie-staffel' in Dutch), which offers indexation if the nominal funding ratio of the fund is above an upper threshold, no indexation if the nominal funding ratio is below a lower threshold, and fractional indexation if it is between the two thresholds. In the numerical results, we set the upper threshold equal to 136% and the lower threshold to 105% a scheme. Intuitively, it is clear that such a scheme is close to a nominal scheme if the current funding ratio is low and the probability that it will ever recover from the low funding ratio is negligible. Equivalently, the scheme will be close to a fully indexed scheme if the funding ratio is high and the asset allocation strategy is such that the funding ratio is unlikely to fall below the upper threshold. This reasoning indicates that the value of the liabilities in such a scheme will depend on the current funding ratio as well as on the asset allocation. Dependence of the value of the liabilities on the asset allocation is at first sight surprising, but is a natural

consequence of the fact that in case of low funding ratios the participants
of the scheme will prefer risk seeking since it can increase their cash flows
while the nominal cash flows are guaranteed anyway.[5] This is not unlike the
preference for participants of an underfunded pension scheme for a risky
asset allocation if the sponsor is obliged to pay for the down-side risk.

We allow for three different choices of the asset mix that includes
nominal bonds with a maturity of 10 years as well as stocks. The initial
nominal funding ratio takes the values 1 and 1.4. The numerical results on
conditional indexation are presented in Table 6.3.

Not surprisingly, Table 6.3 shows that the value of conditionally indexed
schemes is bounded from below by the value of nominal schemes and from
above by the indexed schemes. When the initial funding ratio is low, the
value of conditional indexation is close to the value of the nominal scheme.
After all, the likelihood of ending up in a state in which the liabilities
are indexed is small. The opposite is true when the initial funding ratio
is relatively high, since in that case the conditional indexation scheme in
similar to a fully indexed scheme.

Furthermore, we find for the dependence on the state vector that the
value of conditional indexation is generally increasing in the current level of
inflation and decreasing in the current nominal short rate. The intuition is that
when the current inflation is higher, the liabilities are indexed against a higher
inflation rate in case of indexation, implying that the value of the liabilities
increases. If the nominal short rate increases, the whole nominal and real
term structure increases, which implies that the liabilities are discounted at
a higher rate. This leads to a decrease in the value of the liabilities.

Finally, the value of the liabilities is dependent on the choice of the
asset mix. The rationale is that when the initial funding ratio is low, the
probability of obtaining indexation is low and the conditional indexation
scheme resembles a nominal scheme. Since the value of the liabilities is
not lower in bad states of the world, i.e., when the asset returns are low,
but higher in good states of the world, there is incentive for risk-seeking.
The argument is analogous to standard option pricing theory. In case of a
high initial funding ratio, the value of conditional indexation is lower in bad
states of the world, since the liabilities will not be indexed. In good states
of the world, the value of the liabilities does not change that much, since

---

[5]This paper abstracts from additional complications when there is positive probability that the
sponsor defaults.

Table 6.3.   Value of liabilities when the liabilities are conditionally indexed. Full indexation occurs when the (nominal) funding ratio is higher than 1.36, whereas no indexation is granted whenever the (nominal) funding ratio is lower than 1.05. In between, indexation is provided proportionally. The value of conditionally indexed liabilities is compared to the value of nominal and real liabilities. The actuarial value of the liabilities is equal to 1000. We determine these values for different states of the economy, different initial funding ratios, and different choices of the asset mix. The asset mix selects between stocks and 10 year nominal bonds

Current nom. short rate	Current inflation	Current funding ratio	Fraction stocks	Value conditional indexation	Nom. value liabilities	Real value liabilities
Panel A						
5%	2%	1	0%	740.4		
5%	2%	1.4	0%	895.7		
5%	2%	1	50%	768.1	736.9	914.0
5%	2%	1.4	50%	868.7		
5%	2%	1	100%	780.1		
5%	2%	1.4	100%	840.9		
Panel B						
5%	4%	1	0%	759.1		
5%	4%	1.4	0%	980.5		
5%	4%	1	50%	796.7	755.2	1050.4
5%	4%	1.4	50%	949.3		
5%	4%	1	100%	817.4		
5%	4%	1.4	100%	914.0		
Panel C						
7%	2%	1	0%	647.8		
7%	2%	1.4	0%	776.2		
7%	2%	1	50%	669.4	644.1	788.3
7%	2%	1.4	50%	754.7		
7%	2%	1	100%	679.4		
7%	2%	1.4	100%	731.1		
Panel D						
7%	4%	1	0%	663.1		
7%	4%	1.4	0%	850.9		
7%	4%	1	50%	692.7	658.8	900.3
7%	4%	1.4	50%	823.4		
7%	4%	1	100%	709.9		
7%	4%	1.4	100%	792.5		

indexation occurs already. Consequently, the value of the liabilities is higher when a less risky asset mix is implemented by the pension fund. This implies that the preferred asset mix can be influenced by the liabilities structure of the pension fund.

6.6. Numerical example of the risk management of inflation-sensitive liabilities

In Section 6.3, we have discussed risk management of nominal and indexed liabilities using duration analysis. We emphasized that duration analysis is based on strong assumptions, which are easily shown to be at odds with stylized facts in the data. In particular, duration analysis assumes that long rates are as volatile as short rates and therefore tends to overestimate the interest rate risk of pension schemes. In this section, we indicate how duration analysis can be generalized to the models that are based on less restrictive assumptions as well as to risk management of liabilities that contain derivative components, such as the conditional indexation schemes that have been discussed in Section 6.5. The approach to risk management that is developed in this section can be used e.g. to hedge all risks of specific liability schemes, such as the conditional indexation scheme discussed in Section 6.5. In continuous time settings where markets are complete, this approach leads to replication of the stream of liabilities.

The relative exposure of the market value of an asset or liability with respect to changes of the short term interest rate was the corner stone of the discussion of risk management in Section 6.3. This concept can easily be generalized to the much more general models in Equations (6.16) and (6.17) by considering the relative exposure of the market value of assets with respect to each of the elements of the state vector y_t. Using Equation (6.26) the exposure of the market value of a zero-coupon bond with n periods to maturity with respect to the kth element of the state vector can be written as

$$\varepsilon_k^{(n)} = \frac{1}{P_t^{(n)}} \frac{\partial P_t^{(n)}}{\partial y_{k,t}} = -n \left(b_y^{(n)} \right)_k \tag{6.28}$$

and analogously Equation (6.27) implies for a real bond

$$\varepsilon_k^{R(n)} = \frac{1}{P_t^{R(n)}} \frac{\partial P_t^{R(n)}}{\partial y_{k,t}} = -n \left(b_y^{R(n)} \right)_k \tag{6.29}$$

In order to illustrate the use of Equations (6.28) and (6.29) to generate intuition on the price impact of changes in the state vector note that Table 6.1 implies $\left(b_y^{(10)}\right)_1 = 0.77$, i.e., market value of a nominal zero coupon bond with 10 years to maturity will increase approximately $10 \cdot 0.77\% = 7.70\%$ if the annual real interest rate drops by 1% and the inflation rate is unchanged. The corresponding number for duration analysis is 10%, as duration analysis is simply the special case of Equation (6.28), where the state vector coincides with the annual nominal interest rate and $b_y^{(n)} = 1$ for all n. If both the inflation rate and the annual real interest rate drop by 1% the implied increase in the nominal price of the nominal bond with 5 years to maturity is $5 \cdot (0.89\% + 0.74\%) = 8.15\%$. Likewise, Table 6.2 implies the negative price impact on the equivalent indexed bond will be $5 \cdot 0.89\% = 4.45\%$ if both the nominal rate and inflation increase by 1%.

Like duration analysis, Equations (6.28) and (6.29) cannot only be used to estimate the price impact of changes in the state vector, but can in principle also be used to derive hedging strategies. Consider e.g. an indexed zero-coupon bond with 10 years to maturity. According to Table 6.2, the price of an indexed bond has only an exposure (per unit invested) to the first factor, i.e., the annual real interest decimal rate, of 7.7%. The exposure of a portfolio with $w_1 \cdot 100\%$ of wealth invested in 1 year nominal bonds, $w_5 \cdot 100\%$ of wealth invested in 5 year nominal bonds and $(1 - w_1 - w_5) \cdot 100\%$ of wealth invested in 10 year nominal bonds can easily be verified to equal $w_1 \cdot b_y^{(1)} + 5 \cdot w_5 \cdot b_y^{(5)} + 10 \cdot (1 - w_1 - w_5) \cdot b_y^{(10)}$, with respect to both factors. Substitution of the numerical values from Table 6.1 shows that the exposure of the indexed bond coincides with that of the portfolio of nominal bonds if

$$w_1 \cdot \begin{bmatrix} 1.00 \\ 0.90 \end{bmatrix} + 5 \cdot w_5 \cdot \begin{bmatrix} 0.89 \\ 0.74 \end{bmatrix} + 10 \cdot (1 - w_1 - w_5) \cdot \begin{bmatrix} 0.77 \\ 0.59 \end{bmatrix}$$

$$= 10 \cdot \begin{bmatrix} 0.77 \\ 0 \end{bmatrix} \tag{6.30}$$

Equation (6.30) can easily be solved for w_1 and w_5 which yields $w_1 = 1269.9\%$ and $w_5 = -2617.9\%$. The asset allocation locally hedges all risk factors in the indexed bond under consideration. Since the maturities of the assets and their market values vary over time, a fully replicating strategy would require that the local hedge is adjusted very frequently and that the market is dynamically complete. It should be noted that the hedge portfolio requires rather extreme long and short positions, which can hamper the practical implementation of such a hedge strategy.

In Section 6.5, we have used pricing kernels to derive the market values of liabilities. Once the market is dynamically complete, the valuation on the basis of pricing kernels corresponds to cost of constructing a replicating portfolio. Although our market is not dynamically complete in the discrete time setting, we can determine the composition of the replicating portfolio, pretending that the market is complete. Knowing the market value of each of the components of the indexed scheme, the portfolio that initializes the replicating strategy for the indexed pension scheme can readily be obtained using Equations (6.8) and (6.29), i.e.,

$$\varepsilon_k^{V^R} = \frac{1}{V_t^R} \frac{\sum_{n=1}^{N} \mathbb{E}_t \left(F_{t+n} \right) \partial P_t^{R(n)}}{\partial y_{k,t}}$$

$$= -\frac{1}{V_t^R} \sum_{n=1}^{N} \mathbb{E}_t \left(F_{t+n} \right) n P_t^{R(n)} \left(b_y^{R(n)} \right)_k \tag{6.31}$$

The appendix describes how the $\left(b_y^{R(n)} \right)_k$ coefficients can be obtained from the structural coefficients of the model in Section 6.4. For some specific maturities these parameters have already been reported in Table 6.2. For the cash flow scheme in Figure 6.1, which underlies the numerical example in Section 6.5, the interest and inflation exposure of the indexed scheme can easily be calculated to be $\varepsilon_1^{V^R} = -6107.9$ and $\varepsilon_2^{V^R} = 0$, when the state vector equals its long-term mean. The relative exposures, i.e., the exposures normalized by the value of the indexed liabilities, equals -7.2 for the first factor and 0 for the second factor. By solving a system of two equations in two unknowns like the one in Equation (6.30), one finds that if the true price of the indexed liabilities equals $V_t^R = 848.1$, the hedge portfolio that invests in nominal bonds with maturities of 1 year, 5 year and 10 years has the composition $w_1 = 1197.0\%$, $w_5 = -2452.3\%$ and $w_{10} = 1355.3\%$.

It should be noted that this hedge portfolio is dependent on the current value of the state vector. For example, when the initial state vector equals (7%, 4%, 3%) for the nominal short rate, the annual inflation and excess return in stocks instead of the long-term mean (6%, 2%, 3%), the hedge portfolio changes to $w_1 = 1216.8\%$, $w_5 = -2497.4\%$ and $w_{10} = 1380.5\%$, whereas in case of (5%, 2%, 3%), the hedge portfolio turns out to be $w_1 = 1221.7\%$, $w_5 = -2508.5\%$ and $w_{10} = 1386.8\%$. These portfolios show that the composition of the hedge portfolio is not too volatile given our setting of the parameters and structure of the liabilities. Whether this result carries over to other situations, remains an empirical question.

Until now we restricted ourselves in this section to the case of a fully indexed scheme. In case of non-linear elements in the liability structure, such as the conditional indexation scheme considered in Section 6.5, analytical expressions like Equation (6.31) are no longer available. Nevertheless, the exposures of the market value of conditional indexation schemes to changes in the state vector can easily be determined numerically. Along the lines sketched above, one can therefore easily find the composition of the hedge portfolio that corresponds to such a liabilities structure. However, since the value of the liabilities is now dependent on the funding ratio, the asset mix and the state vector, the hedge portfolio will exhibit these dependencies as well.

Note however that these numbers indicate that significant short sales and substantial trading may be required in the replicating strategy. The implicit assumption that these replicating strategies can be readily and costlessly implemented underlies a large part of the recent literature on modelling the real term structure, on valuation of indexed bonds, and on the utility gains of having access to indexed bonds. Analysis of the possible impact that transaction costs and short sell constraints can have on the replication argument is an important topic for future research.

6.7. Conclusions

In this chapter, we have considered market valuation and risk management of inflation-sensitive pension rights. This topic deserves attention due to the introduction of the new international accounting standards, which requires fair value valuation of both assets and liabilities. In case of nominal or real liabilities, valuation is relatively straightforward. However, indexation schemes have been put in place that provide indexation of pension benefits only in particular states of the world. Valuation of such liabilities is considerably more complicated and introduces new challenges for risk management.

This chapter proposes a framework to value inflation-sensitive liabilities by modelling the pricing kernel in the economy. The specification proposed is in line with the recent affine term structure literature. We discuss how to incorporate different assets, like stocks and nominal bonds, in the menu of assets. Using a stylized model, we illustrate the use of the model in valuing inflation-sensitive pension rights. The model provides interesting insights in the determinants of the fair value of pension liabilities. We find that the asset mix, the initial funding ratio and the current state of the economy, as expressed by the current term structure and inflation rate, can influence the value of the liabilities substantially. Especially the interplay between these factors is highlighted.

Apart from valuation, the model turns out to be particularly useful in risk management applications. First of all, we highlight the assumptions that underlie duration analysis, which is an important risk management tool nowadays in finance practice. By relaxing the assumptions justifying duration analysis, we illustrate the potential errors made by this rule. We discuss in detail how the model proposed can be used in order to come to a better assessment of the risk exposure of inflation-sensitive liabilities.

Several topics are left for future research. In line with the literature, we have assumed throughout that there are no portfolio constraints nor transaction costs. Although practically relevant, incorporation of market frictions is beyond the scope of this chapter. For ease of exposition, we have moreover restricted ourselves to simple models to illustrate the argument. It is well known in the literature that market behavior can be more adequately described by higher order factor models for the term structure of interest rates, more general processes for inflation, as well as time-varying risk premia, see Dai and Singleton (2000, 2003); Campbell and Viceira (2001); Duffee (2002); Ang and Piazzesi (2003); and Sangvinatsos and Wachter (2005). In addition, Ang and Bekaert (2004) argue that regime-switching models are required to model interest rate data properly. Implementation issues of this particular class of models are addressed as well by Ang and Bekaert (2004).

Practical implementation of the model-based valuation and risk management procedures that are advocated in this chapter requires consensus on both the models and parameter values in order to satisfy the requirements of accountants and supervisors. Moreover, a better understanding of model risk, which is inherent to misspecification of aspects of the model, is required. All this is beyond the scope of this chapter.

Appendix A

A6.1. Derivation of the nominal term structure

In this appendix, we show how to derive the parameters of the term structure of interest rates, provided the model outlined in Equations (6.16) and (6.17).

The factors are left unspecified in what follows and can be specialized to the cases discussed in the main text. We assume that the factors that drive the term structure obey a VAR(1)-model

$$x_{t+1} = \mu + \Gamma(x_t - \mu) + \varepsilon_{t+1} \tag{6.32}$$

where $\varepsilon_{t+1} \overset{i.i.d.}{\sim} N(0, \Sigma)$. We assume that both the nominal short rate and inflation are affine in the factors

$$R_t^{(1)} = \delta^\mathsf{T} x_t, \pi_t = \zeta^\mathsf{T} x_t \tag{6.33}$$

Subsequently, we specify the nominal pricing kernel[6]

$$-\log M_{t+1}^\$ = \delta^\mathsf{T} x_t + \frac{1}{2} \beta^\mathsf{T} \Sigma \beta + \beta^\mathsf{T} \varepsilon_{t+1} \tag{6.34}$$

where $\eta_{t+1} \overset{i.i.d.}{\sim} N(0, \sigma_\eta^2)$ and ε_s and η_t are mutually independent for all t and s. The term $\frac{1}{2} \beta^\mathsf{T} \Sigma \beta$ is a Jensen's correction term to ensure that relation (6.14) is valid, i.e.,

$$\mathbb{E}_t \left(M_{t+1}^\$ \cdot 1 \right) = P_t^{(1)} \tag{6.35}$$

which excludes arbitrage opportunities in the economy.

We derive first of all an expression for the risk premium of holding an n period bond for one period. The risk premium is defined by

$$c^{(n)} = \mathbb{E}_t \left(\log P_{t+1}^{(n-1)} - \log P_t^{(n)} \right) - R_t^{(1)} \tag{6.36}$$

i.e., the expected one period holding return in excess of the risk-free rate. It follows from the structure of the model that bond prices are exponentially affine in the factor,[7] i.e.,

$$P_t^{(n)} = e^{-A_{x,n} - B_{x,n}^\mathsf{T} x_t} \tag{6.37}$$

---

[6]In pricing kernel specifications Equations (6.17) and (6.25), the Jensen term $\frac{1}{2} \beta^\mathsf{T} \Sigma \beta$ is denoted by α.

[7]Note that this is indeed a model property. The proof follows by induction and iterating the pricing relation in Equation (6.14).

As a consequence, bond prices and the pricing kernel in Equation (6.34) are jointly log-normally distributed. This implies for Equation (6.36)

$$c^{(n)} = -\frac{1}{2}\text{Var}_t\left(\log P_{t+1}^{(n-1)}\right) - \text{Cov}_t\left(\log P_{t+1}^{(n-1)}, \log M_{t+1}^{\$}\right) \tag{6.38}$$

where we made use of the distributional properties and relation Equation (6.14). Var_t and Cov_t denote respectively the conditional variance and covariance operators. Using the specification in Equation (6.34) and (6.37), we find

$$c^{(n)} = -\frac{1}{2}B_{x,n}^{\mathsf{T}}\Sigma B_{x,n} - B_{x,n}^{\mathsf{T}}\Sigma\beta \tag{6.39}$$

where the first term is a Jensen's correction term.

To determine the coefficients $A_{x,n}$ and $B_{x,n}$, we use the relation in Equation (6.14), where we use the properties of the log-normal distribution. The argument is based on induction and delivers difference equations for both coefficient. Suppose Equation (6.37) is valid up to maturity $n - 1$, then

$$
\begin{aligned}
\log P_t^{(n)} &= \mathbb{E}_t\left(\log P_{t+1}^{(n-1)} + \log M_{t+1}^{\$}\right) \\
&\quad + \frac{1}{2}\,\text{Var}_t\left(\log P_{t+1}^{(n-1)} + \log M_{t+1}^{\$}\right) \\
&= -A_{x,n-1} - B_{x,n-1}^{\mathsf{T}}\left(\mu + \Gamma\left(x_t - \mu\right)\right) - \delta_{x_t}^{\mathsf{T}} - c^{(n)} \\
&= -A_{x,n} - B_{x,n}^{\mathsf{T}}x_t
\end{aligned}
\tag{6.40}
$$

Hence, $A_{x,n}$ and $B_{x,n}$ satisfy

$$A_{x,n} = A_{x,n-1} + B_{x,n-1}^{\mathsf{T}}\left(I - \Gamma\right)\mu + c^{(n)} \tag{6.41}$$

$$B_{x,n} = \Gamma^{\mathsf{T}}B_{x,n-1} + \delta$$

where the difference equations are subject to the initial conditions

$$A_{x,1} = 0, B_{x,1} = \delta \tag{6.42}$$

Note that the difference equation for $B_{x,n}$ is solved by

$$B_{x,n} = \left(I - \Gamma^{\mathsf{T}}\right)^{-1}\left(I - \Gamma^{\mathsf{T}^n}\right)\delta \tag{6.43}$$

Obviously, the coefficients $a_{x,n}$ and $b_{x,n}$ relate to $A_{x,n}$ and $B_{x,n}$ via

$$a_{x,n} = n^{-1}A_{x,n}, b_{x,n} = n^{-1}B_{x,n} \tag{6.44}$$

A6.2. Derivation of the real term structure

The derivation of the real term structure resembles to a large extent the derivation of the nominal term structure. The main difference is the indexation that takes place every period. Formally, the price of a real bond at time t with maturity n is given by

$$P_t^{R(n)} = e^{-A_{x,n}^R - B_{x,n}^{B\mathsf{T}} x_t} \tag{6.45}$$

whereas the payoff is given by

$$P_{t+1}^{R(n-1)} \frac{\Pi_{t+1}}{\Pi_t} \tag{6.46}$$

We define the risk premium on an n period real bond as

$$c^{R(n)} = \mathbb{E}_t \left(\log P_{t+1}^{R(n-1)} + \pi_{t+1} - \log P_t^{R(n)} \right) - R_t^{(1)} \tag{6.47}$$

which can be rewritten along the lines of Equation (6.38) to

$$
\begin{aligned}
c^{R(n)} &= -\frac{1}{2}\text{Var}_t \left(\log P_{t+1}^{(n-1)} + \pi_{t+1} \right) \\
&\quad - \text{Cov}_t \left(\log P_{t+1}^{(n-1)} + \pi_{t+1}, \log M_{t+1}^{\$} \right) \\
&= -\frac{1}{2} \left(B_{x,n-1}^R - \varsigma \right)^{\mathsf{T}} \Sigma \left(B_{x,n-1}^R - \varsigma \right) - \left(B_{x,n-1}^R - \varsigma \right)^{\mathsf{T}} \Sigma \beta
\end{aligned}
\tag{6.48}
$$

In order to determine the coefficients $A_{x,n}^R$ and $B_{x,n}^R$, the same induction argument can be applied, i.e.,

$$
\begin{aligned}
\log P_t^{(n)} &= \mathbb{E}_t \left(\log P_{t+1}^{(n-1)} + \pi_{t+1} + \log M_{t+1}^{\$} \right) \\
&\quad + \frac{1}{2}\text{Var}_t \left(\log P_{t+1}^{(n-1)} + \pi_{t+1} + \log M_{t+1}^{\$} \right)
\end{aligned}
\tag{6.49}
$$

$$= -A^R_{x,n-1} - \left(B^R_{x,n} - \varsigma\right)^\mathsf{T}(\mu + \Gamma(x_t - \mu)) - \delta^\mathsf{T} x_t - c^{R(n)}$$

$$= -A^R_{x,n} - B^{R\mathsf{T}}_{x,n} x_t$$

As a result, we obtain the following difference equations

$$A^R_{x,n} = A^R_{x,n-1} + \left(B^R_{x,n-1} - \varsigma\right)^\mathsf{T}(I - \Gamma)\mu + c^{R(n)} \tag{6.50}$$

$$B^R_{x,n} = \Gamma^\mathsf{T}\left(B^R_{x,n-1} - \varsigma\right) + \delta$$

The boundary conditions are given by

$$A^R_{x,0} = 0, B^R_{x,0} = 0 \tag{6.51}$$

The difference equation for $B^R_{x,n}$ can again be solved in closed form, i.e.,

$$B^R_{x,n} = \left(I - \Gamma^\mathsf{T}\right)^{-1}\left(I - \Gamma^{\mathsf{T}^n}\right)\left(\delta - \Gamma^\mathsf{T}\varsigma\right) \tag{6.52}$$

Finally, we remark that $a^R_{x,n}$ and $b^R_{x,n}$ equal

$$a^R_{x,n} = n^{-1} A^R_{x,n}, b^R_{x,n} = n^{-1} B^R_{x,n} \tag{6.53}$$

References

Ang, A. and G. Bekaert (2004), The Term Structure of Real Rates and Expected Inflation, Paper presented at AFA meeting in San Diego, January 2004.

Ang, A. and M. Piazzesi (2003), "A No-arbitrage vector autoregression of term structure dynamics with macroeconomic and latent variables", *Journal of Monetary Economics,* Vol. 50, No. 4, pp. 745–787.

Brandt, M.W. and D.A. Chapman (2002), Comparing Multifactor Models of the Term Structure, *Working paper.*

Brown, J.R., O. Mitchell and J. Poterba (2001), "The role of real annuities and indexed bonds in an individual accounts retirement program", in: J.Y. Campbell and M. Feldstein, editors, *Risk Aspects of Investment-Based Social Security Reform,* University of Chicago Press, pp. 321–360.

Brennan, M.J. and Y. Xia (2002), "Dynamic asset allocation under inflation", *Journal of Finance,* Vol. 57, No. 3, pp. 1201–1238.

Campbell, J.Y., A.W. Lo and A. Craig MacKinlay (1997), *The Econometrics of Financial Markets,* Princeton University Press.

Campbell, J.Y. and L.M. Viceira (2001), "Who should buy long-term bonds?", *American Economic Review*, Vol. 91, No. 1, pp. 99–127.

Cochrane, J.H. (2001), *Asset Pricing*, Princeton University Press.

Dai, Q. and K.J. Singleton (2000), "Specification analysis of affine term structure models", *Journal of Finance*, Vol. 55, No. 5, pp. 1943–1978.

Dai, Q. and K.J. Singleton (2003), "Term structure dynamics in theory and reality", *Review of Financial Studies*, Vol. 16, No. 3, pp. 631–678.

Deacon, M., A. Derry and D. Mirfendereski (2004), *Inflation-Indexed Securities: Bonds, Swaps, and other Derivatives*, John Wiley & Sons, Inc.

Duffee, G.R. (2002), "Term premia and interest rate forecasts in affine models", *Journal of Finance*, Vol. 57, No. 1, pp. 405–443.

Evans, M. (1998), "Real rates, expected inflation, and inflation risk premia", *Journal of Finance*, Vol. 53, No. 1, pp. 187–218.

Exley, J. (2006), "The Principles of Financial Economics", *this volume*.

Glasserman, P. (2003), *Monte Carlo Methods in Financial Engineering*, Springer, Series: Stochastic Modelling and Applied Probability, Vol. 53.

Hibbert, J., S. Morrison and C. Turnbull (2006), "Techniques for Market-Consistent Valuation of Contingent Claims", *this volume*.

Hull, J. and A. White (1996), *Hull-White on Derivatives*, RISK Publications.

Jarrow, R.A. and S.M. Turnbull (2000), *Derivative Securities*, South-Western College Publishing.

Kortleve, N. and E.H.M. Ponds (2006), "Pension Deals and Generational Transfers", *this volume*.

Sangvinatsos, A. and J.A. Wachter (2005), "Does the failure of the expectation hypothesis matter for long-term investors?", *Journal of Finance*, Vol. 60, No. 1, pp. 179–230.

Fair Value and Pension Fund Management
N. Kortleve, T. Nijman and E. Ponds (Editors)

CHAPTER 7

Fair Value for Pension Fund Liabilities and Consequences for Strategic Asset Allocation

Anthony J. Foley (D.E. Shaw Investment Management, L.L.C.), Andrei Serjantov
(Advanced Research Center, State Street Global Advisors) and Ralph Smith
(Advanced Research Center, State Street Global Advisors)

Keywords: strategic asset allocation, asset liability management, pension funds, surplus optimisation

JEL codes: G11, G23

7.1. Introduction and overview

The recent and growing recognition that liabilities should be measured on a 'fair value' basis has important consequences for the asset allocation of pension funds. This chapter discusses the use of the Merton intertemporal utility-maximisation framework in the context of 'fair' valuation of liabilities. In particular, we introduce and review the model, and discuss its limitations together with the choices of parameters. Finally, we provide a simple 'real world' case study which contrasts the practice of fair valuation of liabilities with the current approach.

7.1.1. Strategic asset allocation

Many of the building blocks of strategic asset allocation theory were put in place by Merton (1969, 1971, 1973) in a series of papers published in the early 1970s. These papers developed the theory of optimal consumption and portfolio allocation in an inter-temporal setting. Optimal portfolios maximise the utility of future wealth accumulated over multiple forward time periods. The approach broadens that of Markowitz by incorporating hedging portfolios which insulate long-horizon investors from changes in the investment opportunity set[1] together with changes in a stochastic risk-free rate.

---

[1] As measured by the ex-ante Sharpe Ratio or market prices of risk of each of the assets.

The presence of these hedging portfolios (whose size is governed by the variability of investment opportunities) means that optimal asset allocations in the Merton specification can be very different from those derived from simple mean-variance optimisation.

Solutions to the intertemporal Merton utility-maximisation are not easy to derive in closed-form except under fairly restrictive assumptions. Numerical solutions have been more successful with approaches including dynamic programming (e.g. Brennan *et al.* (1997)) and discrete-time approximation (e.g. Campbell *et al.* (2001)).

7.1.2. Optimisation in a liability context

The theoretical approach to optimisation in the context where both assets and liabilities are considered has developed somewhat independently of the theory of intertemporal utility-maximisation. In this setting the goal is typically to maximise some function of the surplus (the difference between assets and liabilities). Early work by Sharpe and Tint (1990) set out a practical implementation of the surplus-optimisation approach albeit using a simple, single-period Markowitz optimisation. More recent work has focussed on conducting surplus optimisation in the intertemporal Merton framework for defined benefit plans. Rudolf and Ziemba (2004) set out a version of the Merton model specifically for funds managing in a surplus framework. Detemple *et al.* (2003) developed a new solution for this class of models that is fast enough for practical application of the methodology to defined benefit plans and make it possible to analyse the optimal policy for reasonably complex problems.

It is worth highlighting that a vital component of all surplus optimisation approaches is the measurement of liabilities. The choice of methodology will affect the valuation of liabilities and hence the measured value of the surplus. Optimal asset allocation will be driven (*ceteris paribus*) by the size of the surplus and hence it is critical that liabilities are measured on a fair value basis for the approach to be consistent with a true economic view of the fund's situation.

7.1.3. Current practice in asset allocation

The finance theoretic approach described above contrasts sharply with the asset allocation processes of most pension funds. No two plans approach the strategic asset allocation issue in precisely the same way but there is sufficient commonality for a generic account of current best practice to be useful. For most plans the asset allocation process begins with an actuarial study of the liabilities. This study is used as an input for an allocation analysis which is typically based on mean-variance optimisation.[2] Almost invariably, this exercise is conducted using asset class returns. The resulting allocation is the basis for a second stage process, often referred to as 'risk budgeting.' At this point the process diverges significantly amongst funds. A very few leave it here and actually implement the strategic allocation with a purely passive approach, obtaining the desired asset class returns as cheaply as possible. However, the majority of funds will use a configuration of active, passive and enhanced management across the asset classes. The key risk measure used is often the ex-ante Sharpe ratio, where volatility is measured as tracking error relative to the 'strategic benchmark'.

Bearing in mind the lessons from finance theory, there are in our view, at least three serious concerns in relation to current practice;

- The first is that liability valuation should be based on the fair value principle as discussed above. Surplus is therefore measured consistently with economic value and hence retains equality between the various sets of pension-fund stakeholders
- Liabilities measured in terms of fair value will be stochastic and hence it is unlikely that a strategic benchmark will provide a good proxy, except in the special case where the strategic benchmark itself is the dynamic minimum risk portfolio relative to the liabilities.
- Finally, under the intertemporal Merton approach we should conduct a formal multi-period optimisation rather than rely on a sequence of single-period 'myopic' optimisations. Only by working within a dynamic setting such as this can we attempt to form an asset portfolio which optimally hedges changes in the investment opportunity set or level of expected returns.

In recent years, this dichotomy between theory and practice has potentially been a significant part of the explanation for the wild swings in funding ratios experienced by defined benefit plans. The average funding

---

[2]This mean-variance analysis is increasingly supplemented with Monte Carlo-based stress testing but the analysis remains firmly rooted in a single-period framework.

ratio in the US declined from 116% at the end of 1999 to just 75% at the end of 2002.[3] Since the asset allocation decisions of such plans are often driven by single-period mean-variance optimisation, it may well be that a strategy based on the Merton approach would have delivered better performance over this time period.

An interesting way to compare current best practice to the optimal approach is to calculate the opportunity cost of using the current best practice in situations in which the genuinely optimal policy will give different results and thus calculate the opportunity cost of using an inappropriate solution. This helps the debate in several ways. If the opportunity cost is *de minimis* in most circumstances then this is reassuring for those who believe the current approach is good enough or the best that can be done. Obviously, if there are situations in which the opportunity cost is larger this helps not only clarify whether indeed the current best practice with regard to strategic asset allocation is flawed, but also when those flaws are likely to prove most costly to particular plans.

In this chapter we give a flavour of our model for determining the optimal strategic asset allocation (which, of course, changes over time), emphasising that it is inherently tied to the concept of fair value and then demonstrate by way of an example that naïve 'real world' valuations result in a suboptimal asset allocation. The remainder of the chapter is divided into 4 sections. Section 7.2 introduces the multi-period optimisation model, and Section 7.3 describes the choice of utility function. Section 7.4 provides details on the modelling of liabilities and discusses potential extensions. Finally, Section 7.5 provides a practical example.

7.2. Model description

Two recent papers form the foundation for the model used here. Detemple *et al.* (2003) set out a solution technique for Merton models which is sufficiently fast and flexible to permit the solution of problems of real world complexity. In a working paper, they extend this framework to the surplus management problem. A simpler version of the same framework was published more recently by Rudolf and Ziemba (2004).

---

[3]Source: Watson Wyatt tabulations of Compustat US Disclosure database compiled from SEC filings.

The objective of the investment strategy in the multi-period Merton model is to maximise utility which is derived from intermediate and terminal consumption in excess of that needed to meet liabilities through time. There are a number of potential problems associated with applying such a utility-based approach to a pension fund; we defer the discussion of these, together with the details of the utility functions, to Section 7.3.

The total utility to be maximised is given by:

$$\int_t^T u(c_s - l_s)ds + U(S_T) \tag{7.1}$$

where $u()$ and $U()$ are the intermediate and terminal utility functions, c_t is consumption at time t and the terminal value that is of interest is the surplus S_t, the excess of the terminal portfolio value over terminal liabilities, is defined as:

$$S_t = X_t - L_t \tag{7.2}$$

This consumption profile is financed by an investment portfolio w_t, which along with realised returns determines the evolution of the fund's asset value X_t:

$$dX_t = (X_t r_t - c_t) + X_t w'_t(\mu_t - r_t)dt + \sigma dW_t \tag{7.3}$$

Asset returns and liabilities are conditioned on a set of state variables. Both assets and liabilities for example will be driven by interest rates and inflation. Asset returns are characterised by two sets of stochastic differential equations.

$$dS_{it} = S_{it}(r_t + \sigma_i A_i \Theta_t)dt + S_{it}\sigma_i A_i dW_t \tag{7.4}$$

where S_{it} is the price of asset i at time t, r_t is the risk free rate, σ_i is the volatility of asset i, and $\Theta_t = [\Theta_{1t}, \Theta_{2t}, \ldots, \Theta_{n-1t}, \Theta_{nt}]'$ is the vector of market prices of risk or ex-ante Sharpe ratios for the n assets and $\sigma_i A_i A'_i \sigma'_i$ is the variance covariance matrix of asset returns. These market prices of risk are determined by the second set of stochastic differential equations:

$$d\Theta_{it} = \kappa_{\Theta_i}(\overline{\Theta}_i - \Theta_{it})dt + \sigma_{\Theta_i} dW_t \tag{7.5}$$

where κ_{Θ_i} is the degree to which the ith market price of risk is assumed to revert towards the long-run mean $\overline{\Theta}_i$, and σ_{Θ_i} is the ith row of the matrix of market price of risk volatility coefficients. Note that a mean reverting market price of risk does not imply that returns are mean reverting, merely that risk-premia will oscillate around some equilibrium value.

The other state variables in the model – interest, inflation and wage rates are assumed to be driven by the same risk factors: for instance, inflation follows a mean reverting process where innovations are introduced by the same risk factors that also drive asset returns.

$$dI_t = \kappa_I(\bar{I} - I_t)dt + \sigma_I dW_t \tag{7.6}$$

Liabilities at a point in time can depend in a very general way on the state variables of the model. This allows for a reasonably realistic representation of the liabilities actually faced by defined benefit plans. We do not however model non-market risks such as mortality risk, changes to sponsor or benefit structure etc. Such risks cannot be easily hedged using traditional asset classes and hence we have to rely on actuarial expectations.

Liability value at a point in time is determined by the fair market valuation of anticipated future payouts, which can of course be conditional on the risk factors driving asset returns:

$$L_t = \int_t^T \xi_{t,v}\, l_v\, dv + \xi_{t,T} L_T \tag{7.7}$$

where l_t measures the intermediate value of liabilities at time t and L_T the terminal value of liabilities at time T. These are discussed in more detail in Section 7.4. To obtain the fair valuation, we discount with the state price density (see Hibbert *et al., this volume*, for more details on the state price density valuation):[4,5]

$$\xi_{t,v} = \exp\left[-\int_t^v r_s ds - \int_t^v \Theta_s' dW_s - \frac{1}{2}\int_t^v \Theta_s' \Theta_s ds \right] \tag{7.8}$$

---

[4]We omit some technical conditions here.
[5]Indeed, the discount factors $\xi_{t,v}$ are central to computing both the surplus and the liability parts of the optimal portfolio, for details (of the surplus portfolio calculation) we refer the reader to Detemple *et al.* (2003).

The model is run for some number of years into the future and the outputs are used to compute the optimal portfolio. For technical details we refer the reader to Detemple *et al.* (2003).

The optimal portfolio is made up of four components (see also Rudolf and Ziemba (2004) for a clear exposition of the issues):

1. A liability hedge portfolio.
2. A market portfolio.
3. A state variable hedge portfolio.
4. A riskless asset portfolio.

Perhaps the most important component is the liability hedging portfolio which is exposed to and hedges the risks of the liabilities. It is independent of risk preferences. The remaining three components constitute the surplus portfolio which depends on the risk preferences of the fund. The optimal portfolio can then be expressed as a weighted combination of a preference-free liability portfolio and a preference-dependent surplus portfolio.

7.3. Utility function

The portfolio which we consider optimal is the one which maximises the expression in Equation (7.1). However, we have not yet considered the particular choice of utility functions, nor how they represent the risk preferences of the stakeholders of the pension fund. Let us deal with those two questions in this order.

Following the solution framework in Detemple *et al.* (2003) (extended to the ALM context), we compute the optimal portfolio with respect to two standard utility functions from finance theory – CRRA (Constant Relative Risk Aversion) and HARA (Hyperbolic Absolute Risk Aversion). Each of these is parameterized and hence can be further adapted to the needs of the fund.

The CRRA utility function obeys the property that for all wealth levels c

$$\alpha = -c\frac{u''(c)}{u'(c)} \tag{7.9}$$

and hence the risk aversion stays constant relative to the wealth level.

The HARA utility function is a flexible utility function that permits easy representation of two broad kinds of relationship between funding level and risk aversion. It is given by:

$$u(c) = \frac{(c-b)^{1-R}}{1-R} \tag{7.10}$$

and has relative risk aversion of

$$-c\frac{u''(c)}{u'(c)} = \frac{Rc}{(c-b)} \tag{7.11}$$

So if $b = 0$, relative risk aversion is given by R and is independent of the level of consumption, so for plan sponsors whose risk tolerance is not influenced by their funding ratio, this utility function collapses to the power utility function and exhibits constant levels of relative risk aversion. But for $b > 0$, risk aversion will depend on c and will approach infinity as the floor level of b is approached. This allows for the convenient representation of preferences when the aim is to avoid either the intermediate or terminal value of the surplus falling below a perceived critical level. This might be a level dictated by the institutional framework, for example in the US context the level at which extra insurance payments are payable to the PBGC (Bodie, *this volume*) or it might be an internal target of the fund.

Figure 7.1 illustrates the relationship between the surplus, assets minus liabilities and relative risk aversion for two values of R with a floor at $b = 100$. In both cases, as the surplus tends to zero the level of risk aversion tends to infinity. By comparing the values with $R = 0.25$ and $R = 0.5$, it is apparent that for the former, not only is risk aversion lower for all positive surplus levels but it is also less responsive to changes in the surplus until quite low levels of surplus are reached.

Assuming constant expected returns and risk parameters, the HARA utility function with a floor will generate allocations which are increasing in the risky asset classes as the funding ratio increases, with the sensitivity to changes in the funding ratio greater at funding ratio levels nearer the floor.

Preferences are also likely to vary by plan sponsor and institutional setting when surpluses are negative. Depending on the consequences of underfunded status it could be in the legitimate interest of some stakeholders to have lower risk aversion if the plan is in a chronically under funded condition.

Historical simulation can be a useful part of the likely iterative process of building a model of preferences in a particular case. Once the

Figure 7.1.   *Risk aversion and surplus for the HARA utility function*
with b = 100

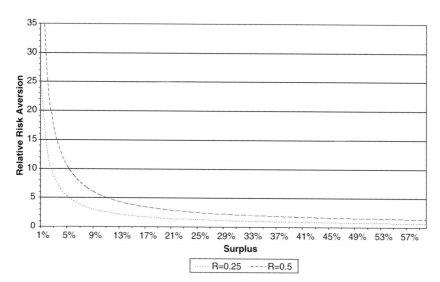

model has been 'calibrated' in this fashion analogous to revealed preference, this part of the model need only be revisited if plan circumstances change markedly.

7.3.1. Problems with the utility maximisation framework

A number of criticisms could be levelled at the set-up of the investment problem as presented above. First of all, one must question the use of a utility function to represent the risk preferences determining the investment decisions of the fund. Indeed one can argue whether such a utility function exists at all (different stakeholders have different horizons and hence one single utility function will not represent them fairly with respect to each other).

Viewing our approach as maximising utility for the average stakeholder of a pension fund may provide more comfort, though it still relies on the fund to make investment decisions with that average stakeholder's utility function in mind (for an excellent discussions of the issues around this, see Campbell and Viceira (2005)).

Secondly, and perhaps most importantly, how can one determine the utility function of the average stakeholder? If it is not possible to determine the appropriate utility function to use in an empirical application then the approach cannot be implemented. There has been considerable criticism of utility based approaches on the grounds that even if they can be justified on positivist grounds for theoretical work, they are not something that can actually be used in practice because people do not know what their utility function is. There is obviously considerable force to this argument, but it is important to remember that what is crucial to obtain are two kinds of information about preferences: the average level of risk aversion and how, if at all, that risk aversion varies with the funding ratio. Plan sponsors, trustees and other stakeholders in funds do not need to be microeconomic theorists to answer such questions, and they are questions which do need to be answered by all funds, whether couched in these terms or not. A historical simulation of the path of the funding ratio, contributions and other key variables can be a very useful tool in helping extract this information from a plan sponsor. Because the liability hedging portfolio is independent of preferences, it is also important not to overstate the importance of the utility function.

7.4. Analysing liabilities

Pension fund liabilities are typically a combination of components which can be either fixed in nominal terms or dependent on other variables: principally wage or retail-price inflation, or contingent in some way on the ability of the fund to provide additional benefits.

The task of valuing liabilities (either known or stochastic) can be conducted in a variety of ways depending on the purpose for which the valuation is required – for an excellent discussion of this see Bodie, *this volume* and Blake (2001). In particular it is very important to distinguish between the economic or fair value of liabilities, and the value derived using the institutional methodologies that apply under given pension law, tax and accounting conventions. Smoothing and formulae that allow some discretion over discount rates place a wedge between the accounting and fair value estimates of liabilities. In some cases the size of this wedge is being reduced by changes in accounting standards designed to bring the two measures more closely into line; it is nevertheless the case that significant differences still exist in the majority of regulatory environments. For the purposes of determining optimal asset allocation we would argue that fair value is the correct approach since only in this way can we measure surplus in a manner such as to preserve equality across the different stakeholders of the fund. See Kortleve and Ponds, *this volume* for a good discussion of how fair valuation allows the identification of potential value transfers between stakeholders resulting from changes in investment policy.

In our model, the liabilities can be dependent on a variety of endogenous variables: inflation, wage rates, interest rates as well as previous liability values. More specifically, the liability model is as follows:

$$l_t = l_{ct} + l_{at}l_{t-1} + l_{lt}\wp(\Theta_t, r_t, I_t, w_t) \tag{7.12}$$

where l_{ct} is a given nominal value for time t, l_{at} is a (potentially) time varying autoregressive component, and $\wp()$ is a function of the current values of the risk factors driving the model, specifically interest rates, inflation and wage rates with l_{lt} a potentially time varying weight on that function. Depending on the problem, terminal liabilities can be calculated as $L_T = l_T$ or can be specified as a separate stochastic process. So in the simplest case with known future nominal liabilities, these would be given by l_{ct} and all other terms would be zero. If future liabilities were sensitive to inflation, then these would be given by l_{lt} and $\wp()$ would be an index function of the inflation rate.

The fair value of the liabilities is then calculated using Equation (7.8). This is consistent with the risk neutral valuation, for details see Hibbert *et al. this volume*. Pricing liabilities in this manner as contingent claims (see also Hibbert *et al. this volume* and Kortleve and Ponds *this volume*) allows for the use of the well developed apparatus of intertemporal asset pricing theory and thus permits much greater flexibility in the modelling of the liabilities and greater clarity to those charged with managing liabilities.

For example, in the Netherlands a new approach allows for indexing of benefits once the funding ratio reaches a certain level. Calculating an optimal solution for a fund in this situation becomes significantly more complicated because the liabilities now depend on the previous-period funding ratio. A high enough value, which leads to indexation will then drive down the fair value estimate of the funding ratio because of the higher liabilities that will likely accrue given indexation. Whilst it is in practice hard to imagine that an optimisation framework will be a complete model of the regulatory environment faced by a pension fund, it is important to ensure that the assumptions in the optimisation are a reasonably close approximation to the underlying reality of the fund. Contingent liability considerations in particular are certainly material enough to potentially influence the optimal allocation.

While this does complicate matters somewhat, it is of course the case that in an integrative framework, the speed advantage relative to a conventional asset-liability modelling exercise is so overwhelming that it is very plausible to run the analysis under different assumptions about the liability process. The effect of changes in assumptions on estimated surplus and optimal asset allocation can then be directly evaluated.

A similar statement can be made about the contributions. For instance, in the US market, there is a set of rules as to when the pension fund sponsor, (usually the parent company) has to provide additional contributions to the pension fund in order to reduce the deficit (underfunding). As in the case with indexation, pricing these potential contributions presents a challenge, but the framework at least allows us to easily consider different scenarios (best and worst case, for instance) if not the 'actual case.'

7.5. Case study

The model specified in Equations (7.1) through (7.7) and (7.10) can be solved by an innovative Monte Carlo approach based on the Malliavin calculus. The solution technique is covered extensively in Detemple *et al.* (2003).

As with any contingent claims analysis, the model needs to be calibrated and in this case the inputs that need calibration are the covariance matrices of asset price returns and liabilities and the market prices of risk, and the mean reversion parameters driving the dynamics of both assets and liabilities. Some of these parameters are difficult to recover from a purely data based approach to estimation. In particular, it is heroic to attempt to estimate the mean reversion parameters from anything but extremely long data sets which will not typically be available. So in the absence of such data sets, a mixed estimation procedure will typically be prudent. The approach here is to specify the mean-reversion parameters exogenously and then calibrate the model to historical data conditional on these mean-reversion parameters.

In this example we present a typical analysis for a European pension fund wishing to utilise the approach described above to make their strategic asset allocation decisions. This requires the calculation of an optimal portfolio for a range of funding ratios, with respect to their assumed utility function. In practice this would then be used to rebalance the asset allocation accordingly at regular intervals. In order to calibrate the fund's risk tolerance and infer a utility specification, we assume the Netherlands regulatory environment applies.[6]

In this example we have used the following asset classes:

- Domestic Government Bond Index, 10+ Years (Euro)
- Domestic Index Linked Bond Index (Euro)
- Domestic Equity Index (Euro)
- Foreign Equity Index Hedged (World ex Europe)
- Alpha (an index representing hedge-fund performance)
- Domestic Real Estate Index
- Emerging Market Equity Index
- Foreign Equity Index Unhedged (World ex Europe)
- Domestic Corporate Bond Index

It is worth noting that the various asset classes are modelled slightly differently to each other: the stochastic process representing the market price of risk of the bond index is driven by the same source of randomness as the interest rate, the same holds for index linked bonds and inflation; the other prices are modelled separately.

In this example, we assume the following nominal liability profile (see Figure 7.2).

We now proceed to contrast the approaches to valuing the liabilities. We have distilled the discussion above to two common cases: the current commonplace practice of using a fixed or actuarially smoothed discount rate, and the 'fair value' approach, which uses the state price density as in Equation (7.8). Finance theory does not offer us an optimal portfolio in the former case, hence we model the 'current practice' as an optimal portfolio in the intertemporal framework, but computed based on an actuarially smoothed and thus *ad hoc* liability measure. Such cases are commonly encountered in practice. Hence, our comparison of the 'fair value' vs. the traditional approach to liability estimation is somewhat simple, with the only difference between the two cases being the value of the liabilities and hence the surplus.

The second issue resulting from the valuation of liabilities is that the current approach which uses a constant discount rate is usually implemented with a static portfolio while the optimal portfolio in the 'fair value' case is

---

[6]See, for example the FTK consultation document, 21 October 2004 (www.dnb.com).

A.J. Foley, A. Serjantov and R. Smith

Figure 7.2.   Liability profile

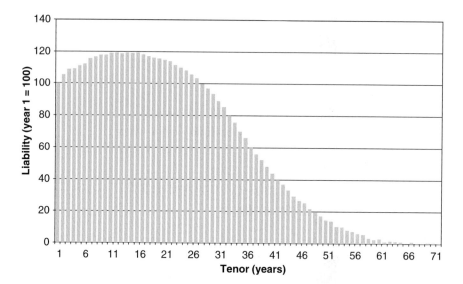

clearly a dynamic one.[7] We contrast these two approaches by the use of a Monte Carlo simulation.

The utility function used in this example is a very simple CRRA specification with the risk aversion set to represent a reasonable view of the pension fund stakeholders' tolerance for risk. In practice, the process of defining a utility function for a fund is typically an iterative one; preferences expressed over different portfolios at various wealth levels can form the basis of an informed decision.

The following chart (Figure 7.3) shows the optimal portfolio composition under the 'fair valuation' of liabilities for a range of different funding ratios. Note that the Alpha allocation is constrained at a maximum of 10% and the Emerging Market Equity allocation is constrained at a maximum of 15%; these constraints are reflective of current common practice.

As we mentioned before, measuring the liabilities in a 'fair value' sense and in the 'current practice' actuarial sense will likely produce significantly different values of the liability and hence surplus. Even if the valuation of the liabilities only influences the size of the surplus (here we suppose

---

[7]Actually, even if the portfolio is targeted against a static benchmark rather than the liabilities, the optimal portfolio in the utility maximising sense (see Detemple *et al.* (2003)) changes over time, but such an approach is rarely used in practice.

Figure 7.3. Optimal portfolio with 'fair value' discounting

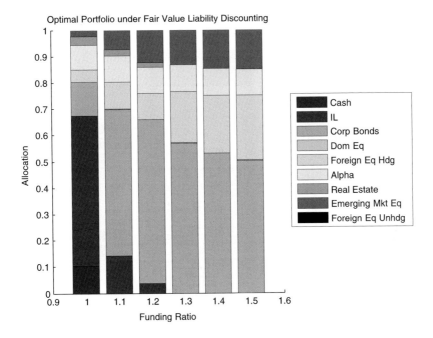

a difference of approximately 1% in the discount rate) and the rest of the optimal portfolio calculation is left as is, the composition of the two resultant portfolios is rather different. In the constant discount case, the surplus is significantly larger and hence substantially more risk is taken as shown in Figure 7.4. Measuring the surplus differently and optimising accordingly results in an equity allocation around 15% greater than the 'fair value' case. Such an allocation difference is likely to be considered very significant by a typical pension fund.

The current practice of discounting of liabilities with a single fixed or smoothed actuarial rate naturally leads to the use of a static strategic benchmark. The portfolios which are constructed to achieve or out-perform such benchmarks are typically similarly static or constant-mix, e.g. '35% Equities and 65% Bonds.' On the other hand once we accept the idea of using the 'fair' approach to valuation of liabilities in the context of a surplus management framework, it is natural for the asset allocation to be dynamic. In the following simulation we compare the performance of a static portfolio to that of the (approximation to) optimal portfolio for 10 years into the future in the context of 'fair valuation' of liabilities. More specifically, we compare the

Figure 7.4. Comparing 'optimal' portfolios under different liability valuations

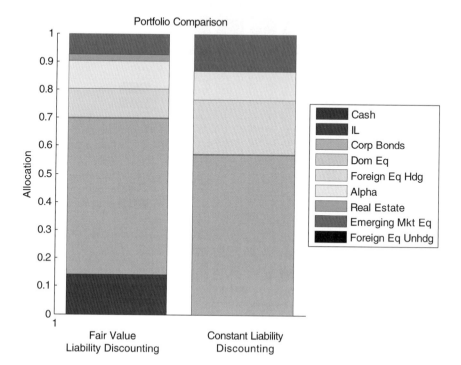

optimal portfolio of Figure 7.3 with two sample portfolio specifications – a 35/65 Equity/Bonds mix representative of the current industry average and a diversified static portfolio representing the output of a single-period mean-variance optimisation.[8] The comparison was obtained by means of a Monte Carlo simulation using a similar asset-price model as described in Section 7.2.

Figure 7.5 below shows the distribution of funding ratios of the dynamic optimal portfolio and the 35/65 mix after 10 years.

In Table 7.1 below we report the results for the dynamic multi-period optimal portfolio compared with both the 35/65 Equity/Bond mix and the diversified static portfolio. It is clear from both Figure 7.5 and Table 7.1 that the distributions of funding ratios resulting from static and dynamic

---

[8]The composition of this portfolio is; 42% Bonds, 19.1% Domestic Eq, 11.5% International Eq, 10.3% Corporate Bonds, 9.6% Property, 6.7% Emerging Mkt Eq.

Figure 7.5.   *Funding ratio comparison after 10 years*

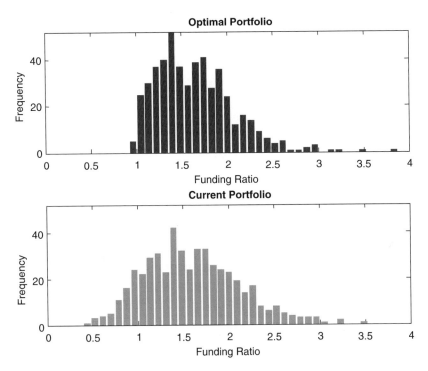

Table 7.1.   *Performance of static and dynamic portfolios*

	Optimal Portfolio	35/65 Equity/Bond Portfolio	Diversified Portfolio
Mean FR	1.6442	1.5928	1.6854
STD FR	0.4336	0.5215	0.6378
Pr(FR <1.2)	0.152	0.246	0.232
Pr(FR <1.1)	0.066	0.178	0.176
Pr(FR <1.05)	0.04	0.16	0.162
Pr(FR <1.0)	0.01	0.128	0.136

portfolios are very different, the latter having much more desirable characteristics. In particular, we see that the dynamic optimal portfolio has
significantly lower variance and probability of underfunding compared to
the 35/65 portfolio mix, whilst delivering a higher realised return. Clearly,
this is a direct consequence of adopting a surplus optimisation approach in
general and the multi-period optimal portfolio in particular.

The above analysis provides reassuring empirical support to the optimality of the dynamic multi-period solution. From a practical point of view, this conclusion suggests that pension funds switching to the 'fair value' approach should also consider adopting a dynamic approach to the asset liability management problem. The reduction in the probability of underfunding generated from following such dynamic policies fits neatly into the risk-control based frameworks currently being adopted by the DNB in the Netherlands, and by other regulatory bodies across Europe.

7.6. Conclusions

In this chapter we looked at how fair valuation of liabilities impacts asset allocation decisions of pension funds. We presented a framework which allows us to compute optimal portfolios in a multi-period utility maximisation sense and showed that the usual constant or smoothed discount-rate approach to valuing the liabilities results not only in a suboptimal, but also a substantially different portfolio. We next looked at how both typical and diversified static portfolios perform against the optimal dynamic portfolio in a Monte Carlo simulation when 'fair' valuation of liabilities is used. The results show that the optimal portfolio significantly lowers the probability of underfunding in 10 years time.

The fair value approach to liability estimation dovetails nicely with newer integrative approaches to strategic asset allocation for pension funds. Better planning requires better tools. The development of the 'fair value' approach is timely and will support plan sponsors' efforts to align their asset allocation and liability profile more appropriately. Our analysis suggests that a switch to a fair value framework for liabilities would likely have a meaningful asset allocation impact relative to the simplest alternative of discounting using a constant rate. However, a very important benefit of the integrative approach is that the links between assumptions and allocations become far more transparent. In particular, the decomposition of the portfolio into a liability benchmark and surplus portfolio provides a very useful and straightforward way of measuring and managing the investment and liability risk inherent in pension portfolios.

Bibliography

Blake, D. (2001), UK Pension Fund Management: How is Asset Allocation Influenced by the Valuation of Liabilities? Pension Institute Discussion Paper 0104.

Bodie, Z. (2006), "The Fair Value Accounting and Pension Benefit Guarantees", *this volume*.

Brennan, M., E. Schwartz and R. Lagnado (1997), "Strategic asset allocation", *Journal of Economic Dynamics and Control*, Vol. 21, pp. 1377–1403.

Campbell, J.Y., Y.L. Chan and L.M. Viceira (2001), A Multivariate Model of Strategic Asset Allocation. NBER Working Papers 8566, National Bureau of Economic Research.

Campbell, J.Y. and L.M. Viceira (2005), "Strategic asset allocation for pension plans", in: G. Clark, A. Munnell and M. Orszag, editors, *Oxford Handbook of Pensions and Retirement Income*, Oxford University Press.

Detemple, J.R., R. Garcia and M. Rindisbacher (2003), "A Monte Carlo method for optimal portfolios", *Journal of Finance*, Vol. 58, pp. 401–446.

Exley, J. (2006), "The Fair Value Principle", *this volume*.

Hibbert, J., S. Morrison and C. Turnbull (2006), "Techniques for Market-Consistent Valuation of Contingent Claims", *this volume*.

Kortleve, N.E. and E.H.M. Ponds (2006), "Pension Deals and Value-based ALM", *this volume*.

Merton, R.C. (1969), "Lifetime portfolio selection under uncertainty: The continuous-time case", *Review of Economics and Statistics*, Vol. 51, pp. 247–257.

Merton, R.C. (1971), "Optimum consumption and portfolio rules in a continuous time model", *Journal of Economic Theory*, Vol. 3, pp. 273–413.

Merton, R.C. (1973), "An intertemporal capital asset pricing model", *Econometrica*, Vol. 41, pp. 867–887.

Rudolf, M. and W.T. Ziemba (2004), "Intertemporal surplus management," *Journal of Economic Dynamics and Control*, Vol. 28, pp. 975–990.

Sharpe, W.F. and L.G. Tint (1990), "Liabilities - a new approach", *Journal of Portfolio Management*, Vol. 16, No. 2, pp. 5–11.

PART III

Application

Fair Value and Pension Fund Management
N. Kortleve, T. Nijman and E. Ponds (Editors)
© 2006 Elsevier B.V.

CHAPTER 8

Fair Value Accounting and Pension Benefit Guarantees

Zvi Bodie (Boston University School of Management)

Fair value accounting is essential for the protection of plan beneficiaries. When the government is the ultimate guarantor of pension promises, fair value accounting is also essential for the protection of the taxpayers, who ultimately must bear the costs of pension asset shortfalls in the defined-benefit system. In the US the government has been insuring private pension plans through the Pension Benefit Guaranty Corporation (PBGC) since 1974. In the UK a similar entity called the Pension Protection Fund, was created in 2004. Even in the Netherlands, where there are no formal government guarantees of pension plan promises, it is probably correct to assume that the government would step in and assume some of the liability in the event of a serious default. Like banks, pension funds are simply 'too important to fail.'

In this chapter, I will start by analyzing the role of guarantees of private sector pensions. Then I will describe the system for guaranteeing defined-benefit pensions in the United States, and will demonstrate the critical role that misleading accounting practices have played in weakening that system and bringing it to a crisis point. I conclude with some observations on the implications for other pension systems.

8.1. The role of pension benefit guarantees

A major putative advantage of a defined-benefit pension plan over a defined contribution plan is that it protects the employee against invest-ment risk. The economic efficiency of this protection against investment risk is enhanced by the provision of guarantees against default risk. To understand the efficiency gains from guarantees of pension annuities, it is critical to distinguish between the employees and investors (stockholders and bondholders) in firms that provide pension annuities. The distinction is that unlike the firm's stockholders, the employees holding the sponsor's pension liabilities strictly prefer to have the payoffs on their contracts as insensitive as possible to the default risk of the firm itself. The function served by a pension annuity is for the beneficiaries to receive a specified benefit upon retirement. That function is less efficiently performed if the contract instead calls for the benefit to be paid in the joint event that the employee retires *and* the firm is still solvent.

Even if the sponsoring firm offers an actuarily-fair increase in the employee's cash wages to reflect the risk of insolvency, it is still likely that an employee would prefer a pension annuity with the least default risk. Employees typically have a large non-diversified stake in the firm already. They may have invested in firm-specific human capital, which loses value if the firm does poorly. Thus few employees would consciously agree to accept default risk on their pension benefits in order to increase their cash wages. This is true even when the employee has all of the relevant information necessary to assess the default risk of the firm. In most cases the employees do not have the relevant information, and this fact makes the welfare loss even worse.

For example, consider the profile of a 'typical' defined-benefit plan beneficiary. The vast majority are blue-collar and white-collar workers for whom pension benefits constitute a large portion of total retirement savings. These employees are very unlikely to have asset portfolios of sufficient size or the investment expertise necessary to hedge the non-diversifiable risks of their defined-benefit pension asset. Only the most highly compensated managerial employees of the firm might have the total assets and knowledge required to diversify away the risks of their defined-benefit pension claims. But to hedge this risk, they would have to effectively take a short position in the sponsoring firm's equity. Typically, managers and employees are prohibited from short-selling the firm's securities by the provisions of their incentive compensation package.

By contrast, an investor in the stocks or bonds issued by the sponsoring firm is explicitly taking an interest in the fortunes of the firm itself. The function of these securities is to allow investors to participate in the risk and return prospects of the firm. Investors can diversify away much of the default risk associated with any one specific firm as part of their total portfolios. Employees with a substantial part of their wealth in firm-specific defined-benefit pension annuities usually cannot achieve such optimal diversification. They are like investors who are constrained to hold a large fraction of their wealth in the form of long-term bonds issued by a single firm, which is also their employer. Thus, both their tangible and human capital are significantly exposed to the fortunes of a single firm.

Note that the risk exposure is especially large for a lifetime employee of a single firm. Even if the employee is willing to bear risk, we know from portfolio theory that efficient risk-bearing calls for broad diversification across various firms and asset classes. Here, the employee's entire pension benefit is tied to the fortunes of a single firm. Should employees wish to invest in the securities of their firm, they typically can do so through a variety of special employee stock ownership programs. These investment programs are usually voluntary.

A firm sponsoring a defined-benefit pension plan can provide assurances against default risk to plan beneficiaries in three different ways:

1. By funding the plan or assuring that plan beneficiaries have a priority claim to the firm's non-pension assets. Thus even employees of a firm with an unfunded pension plan can be protected against default risk of their pension benefits if there are adequate non-pension assets and the other stakeholder claims against the sponsoring firm's assets are clearly subordinated in the event of bankruptcy.
2. By purchasing guarantees of its pension liabilities from a private-sector third party. In the United States, private guarantees of a sponsor's pension liabilities are generally not available as such. However, some sponsors contract with insurance companies to provide pension annuities, thus effectively making the insurance company the guarantor of those benefits. If the solvency of the insurance company is in question, however, then the goal of guaranteeing employee pension benefits is not completely achieved.
3. Through government guarantees of its pension liabilities.

The basic methods that any guarantor (whether private-sector or government) has to manage its business on a sound basis are:

- *Funding Requirements:* Set standards for the full funding of promised benefits (i.e., 'capital adequacy' and act swiftly to limit losses when these funding standards are violated (i.e., avoid 'forbearance').
- *Matching Restrictions:* Require the insured entity to hedge its insured liabilities by matching the market-risk exposure of its assets to its insured liabilities.

- *Pricing:* Set a premium schedule for the guarantee commensurate with the guarantor's exposure to the risk of a shortfall.

8.1.1. The case of the PBGC in the United States[1]

To understand the importance and potential impact of fair value reporting of corporate pension assets and liabilities it is instructive to consider the case of the Pension Benefit Guarantee Corporation in the United States.

The PBGC insures the pension benefits of the 44 million Americans covered by private defined-benefit pension plans. Traditional pension plans of the defined-benefit type have been declining in relative importance in recent years. Companies are (legally) terminating them and replacing them with 'defined-contribution' plans such as 401(k) plans that amount to tax-deferred private savings plans. The number of private defined-benefit plans peaked in the mid-1980s at 112,000. At that time, about 40 percent of American workers were covered by them. Over the past two decades, the number of plans has fallen to just over 31,000 plans, which cover only one worker in five. No large companies have started defined-benefit plans in recent years.

Most existing defined-benefit plans are sponsored by a single company, but there are also multi-employer plans that cover workers at several firms in the same industry. These multi-employer plans, such as the Teamsters' Central States Pension Fund, are run by boards typically representing a trade union and the companies that employ the union's members. The PBGC insures both single-employer and multi-employer plans, but the terms of the insurance are different. The single-employer insurance system is by far the larger of the two and has a much larger deficit.

When a PBGC-insured pension plan is terminated with insufficient assets to pay the benefits promised to employees – typically, by an employer bankruptcy – the PBGC takes it over and makes up the shortfall. There is a cap on the insured benefit, however, which is currently $45,000 per year.

8.2. How the PBGC is financed

By law, the PBGC is supposed to finance all of its operations from three sources: (1) the premiums it collects from companies that still sponsor

---

[1]This section is based on my article, 'Straight Talk About Government Pension Insurance,' Milken Institute Review, February 2005.

defined-benefit plans, (2) the assets it recovers from terminated underfunded plans and (3) from the interest, dividends and capital gains it earns on its accumulated reserves. Premiums come from a charge to plan sponsors of $19 per single-employer plan participant and $2.60 for multi-employer participants. There is also a variable premium charged to single-employer sponsors with significant underfunding. The charge is $9 per $1000 of unfunded vested benefits.

Significantly, the funding requirements and premiums charged by the PBGC are completely unrelated to the way pension assets are invested. A plan sponsor with 100% invested in equities has the same funding require-ment and pays the same premium as a sponsor with 100% in fixed income securities.

The PBGC's own investment policies have varied over the years. In 2004 the PBGC announced it will try to better-match its assets and liabilities by increasing its investment in fixed income securities with cash flows similar to its expected payments.

PBGC is effectively the successor trustee for plans it takes over and it acts as a creditor in this capacity. Although there are exceptional circumstances where PBGC has a higher recovery priority, it generally acts as an unsecured creditor, at the bottom of the bankruptcy priority list.

Most informed observers believe that ultimately the US Treasury – i.e., taxpayers – will have to bail out the PBGC, just as it bailed out the govern-ment agency that insured savings & loan association accounts in the 1980s.

8.2.1. How big might the bailout be?

In its annual report, the PBGC presents a balance-sheet measure called 'net position,' which amounts to its assets minus its liabilities evaluated at current market prices. The liability figure is the present value of the future benefits that have already become or are about to become an obligation of the PBGC as a result of bankrupt underfunded plans. If this net position is negative, it is a rough estimate of the extra money the PBGC would have to set aside today in the form of income-producing assets to satisfy all claims. It is therefore a good indicator of the magnitude of the possible bailout.

On November 15, 2004 the PBGC released its annual report for fiscal year 2004, which ended on September 30. It contains a financial summary showing the net position for each program – single employer and multi-employer – going back to 1995. (see Figure 8.1 below).

Figure 8.1. PBGC's net financial position

Year	1995	1996	1997	1998	1999	2000	2001	2002	2003	2004
Single-employer	−0.315	0.869	3.481	5.012	7.038	9.704	7.732	−3.638	−11.238	−23.305
Multi-employer	0.192	0.124	0.219	0.341	0.199	0.267	0.116	0.158	−0.261	−0.236
Both combined	−0.123	0.993	3.7	5.353	7.237	9.971	7.848	−3.48	−11.499	−23.541

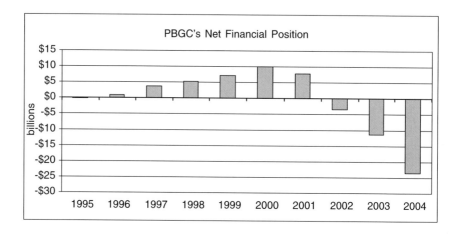

The trend is negative in both the single-employer program and the multi-employer program, but the magnitude of the problem is much larger in the former. In 1996 the single-employer program's net position was positive – i.e., in surplus – and it stayed positive until 2001 when it reached $7.7 billion. But in the last three years, the ink has turned decidedly red: the deficit now stands at $23.3 billion.

This deficit could get much bigger. As of the end of the 2004 fiscal year, the PBGC's estimate of the underfunding in plans sponsored by companies with credit ratings below 'investment grade' – that is, at significant risk of default – was $96 billion. But even the $96 billion figure for struggling companies is not the upper limit on the possible deficit. PBGC estimates that the total underfunding in single-employer plans exceeded $450 billion, while multi-employer plans were under water to the tune of $150 billion. The US economy is now in pretty good shape, and well-financed companies that sponsor underfunded plans will probably be able to make up their pension plan shortfalls without help from the PBGC. But if there is another serious economic downturn, the number of distressed companies with underfunded pension plans could grow dramatically.

8.2.2. Valuing the PBGC deficit using option pricing methodology

Federal pension insurance can be valued as a compound option to put the assets of a defined benefit pension plan to the government at a price equal to the value of insured pension liabilities, contingent on the insolvency of the sponsoring firm. Applying options pricing methods to recent information on the financial condition and other characteristics of plans and their sponsors, the US Congressional Budget Office (CBO) estimates that the total shortfall and hence the cost exposure of the government for federal pension insurance provided through the Pension Benefit Guaranty Corporation is currently about $135 billion.[2] This total consists of two distinct components: losses from insurance claims for plans that have already terminated or whose termination is anticipated and, thus, is effectively unavoidable and has already been recognized by PBGC ($23.3 billion); and prospective losses for terminations that have not yet occurred net of future premiums ($111.7 billion).

CBO's $111.7 billion forward-looking net cost estimate is much higher than the PBGC's estimate of $16.9 billion for probable losses. The difference is that the options pricing approach includes losses arising from firms that will become financially distressed in the future, not only firms that already are in severe financial distress. At the same time, the $111.7 billion is only slightly higher than the PBGC's estimate of reasonably possible losses of $96 billion. There are two offsetting effects on the relative size of these two measures. Reasonably possible losses include the entire amount of current under-funding of firms with below investment grade credit ratings, many of which are likely to remain in business long enough to substantially reduce their funding gaps. On the other hand, the estimate of reasonably possible losses neglects the possibility that currently healthy firms will default in the future, and that the losses from currently distressed firms may grow larger.

8.3. Anatomy of the crisis

The current crisis did not follow from some perfect storm of unforeseeable factors. I know this from personal experience: In the early 1990s I was hired by the Department of Labor to analyze the financial health of defined-benefit pension plans.

---

[2]This is according to a report published by the US Congressional Budget Office in April 2005, 'Estimating and Controlling PBGC's Risk Exposure.'

I concluded that there was a fundamental mismatch between the liabilities of these plans – future pension payouts – and the assets in which they were investing their reserves. This mismatch meant that even plans that were fully funded at the time could quickly become underfunded as a result of changes in interest rates or stock prices.

I submitted my report to the Department of Labor's Pension and Welfare Benefits Administration, and briefed the executive director of the PBGC on my findings. I also made my conclusions known in the professional community. In an article published in the *Journal of Financial Services Research* in 1996 – a time when the PBGC and most of the plans it insures had comfortable surpluses – I warned:

> The possible 'doomsday' scenario for the defined-benefit pension system would be an event such as a sharp and prolonged drop in stock prices that causes a sharp decline in the market value of pension asset portfolios. Underfunding becomes much more prevalent. Several major defaults of underfunded pension plans lead the PBGC to significantly raise premiums on the remaining plans in the system.
>
> Expectations of even higher premiums in the future lead sponsors of the well-funded plans to terminate their defined-benefit plans to avoid the PBGC 'tax.' They buy annuities to settle all benefits accrued under the terminated plans and replace them with generous defined-contribution plans, thus avoiding criticism from their employees or from the public. Ultimately, the United States could be left only with bankrupt defined-benefit plans with the benefits financed directly by taxpayers.

Today, the PBGC appears to have been sucked into that doomsday scenario. Why was my warning, which was solicited by the government itself, so casually ignored?

The answer has its roots in a fundamentally flawed belief about the nature of stock-market risk and reward, a belief that still guides the thinking and the practices of the vast majority of professional pension actuaries and investment advisors. It is the proposition that although stocks are a risky investment in the short run, they are a safe bet in the long run.

This mistaken proposition leads financial professionals to advise their corporate clients that they can significantly reduce the cost of funding their long-term obligations to defined-benefit plans by investing in diversified portfolios of stocks instead of matching the liabilities with a portfolio of bonds that deliver specified sums of cash at specified times.

The accounting profession has codified this fallacy in the way it treats pension expenses in company statements of profit and loss. Indeed, under current rules, if a company should choose to invest pension assets in bonds whose future cash inflows exactly match the pension benefits, the company would have to report higher pension expenses and lower profits than would an identical company that invested in stocks.

So what exactly is the fallacy? Consider a very simple example. Assume that ABC company has a defined-benefit plan for a single employee, Jane Jones. Jane has worked for the firm for a year, and as a result has earned the right to a pension payment of $1000 when she retires 20 years from now. If the interest rate on bonds maturing in 20 years is 5 percent per year, the company would have to invest $376.89 in such bonds today in order to be certain to have $1000 in 20 years to pay to Jane. Under US pension law, the bonds would be held by a pension trust, so that even if ABC were to go bankrupt Jane would still receive her promised benefit.

The $376.89 is the 'present value' of the promised future pension benefit, and accounting logic dictates that it is the amount of ABC's pension expense in the current year. In each subsequent year, no matter what happens to interest rates or stock prices, the value of the bond will exactly match the pension liability. Underfunding is impossible in these circumstances (as long as the ability of the bond issuer to pay its debts was in no doubt), and the PBGC will never have to pay a dime to Jane.

But ABC's pension consultant insists that ABC consider an alternative. Because the pension payment is not due for another 20 years, ABC has the option of investing in stocks to earn an expected rate of return of 10 percent per year – a plausible figure based on past stock market returns. Sure, from year to year stock prices will fluctuate, but over two decades the ups and downs will cancel out. If it sets aside $376.89 for Jane's pension, ABC could – in fact, should – record a profit on the difference between the 10 percent long-run expected rate of return on stocks and the 5 percent interest rate on the accruing pension benefit.

What is wrong with this reasoning? Fluctuations in stock prices do not necessarily cancel out over time, no matter how long the time period. And contrary to the conventional actuarial reasoning, the risk of falling short of the target is actually *greater* in the long run than in the short run.

To see why, one need only check how much it would cost for ABC to buy insurance against such a shortfall. (The policy would make up the difference between $1000 and the value of the stocks in the pension portfolio.) Both in finance theory and in practice, the price of such insurance (called a put option) increases with the length of the time horizon.[3]

---

[3] See the appendix for a more complete explanation.

In our example, the cost of insuring against a shortfall if the stock portfolio is worth less than $1000 in 20 years would be about $125. So to keep the upside potential of the stock portfolio and still be certain that at least $1000 would be available to pay Jane, ABC would have to lay out $125 in addition to the $376.89 invested in stocks. And this is assuming that all dividends from the stocks are reinvested. So investing in stocks instead of bonds does not lower the cost of the promised pension benefit unless Jane is obliged to bear the risk of not receiving it – or unless the PBGC is there to pick up the extra cost of guaranteeing the pension payout.

8.4. Similarities with FSLIC

There are some significant similarities between the United States government system for guaranteeing pension benefits and the failed system for insuring savings and loan associations (S&Ls). The Federal Savings and Loan Insurance Corporation (FSLIC) was the government agency that insured the S&Ls until it was replaced in 1989.

In the environment of stable interest rates that prevailed throughout the 1950s and 1960s, everyone viewed S&Ls as very safe institutions. The problems began in the 1970s when interest rates became high and volatile. Even S&Ls that held well-diversified portfolios of mortgages became insolvent in the environment of rising interest rates of the 1970s because the mortgages were long term and fixed-rate while their deposit liabilities were short-term and rolled over at increasingly higher market rates. Still more S&Ls became insolvent in the late 1980s because the real estate market collapsed. Thus *both* of the market risks to which S&Ls were exposed – interest rate risk and real estate risk – took their toll. The biggest losses to FSLIC were incurred not as a result of fraud or even of poorly diversified asset portfolios, but rather as a result of failure on the part of regulators to act quickly to stem the losses resulting from the asset-liability mismatch.

In the case of the PBGC, the nature of the liabilities of private defined-benefit pension plans is very different from the short-term deposit liabilities that were insured by FSLIC. Therefore, the type of assets which match those liabilities is different. The similarity is that in both cases, there is a mismatch between the market-risk exposures of the assets and liabilities that exposes the government guarantor to substantial shortfall risk.

The expressed purpose of establishing the PBGC was to insure a minimum level of promised defined benefit pensions against default risk of the plan sponsor. However, if firms can transfer their pension obligations to the

PBGC, then the government effectively pays a portion of the workers' total compensation because these obligations are linked to workers' pay. The size of this government subsidy can be large. Similarly, PBGC insurance has served in a less visible way to guarantee the debt of financially troubled firms than guaranteeing the bonds issued by these firms.

8.5. What to do

Those who created the present mess are blaming a perfect storm of stagnant stock prices, low interest rates and industrial restructuring for the PBGC's problems, as if nothing could have been done to prepare. But it is worth noting that many of the pension plans that are weak today were fully funded in the late 1990s. Had they hedged their exposure to a decline in interest rates at that time, they would have easily survived the subsequent storm intact.

Since the creation of the PBGC, many companies have terminated their defined-benefit plans and replaced them with less expensive defined-contribution plans, thereby shifting the risk that retirement portfolios will produce disappointing returns to retirees. Ironically, one incentive for doing this is the existence of PBGC insurance in its current form. The current system overcharges sponsors of healthy plans in order to subsidize the ailing ones. Thus we have a classic case of the Law of Unintended Consequences: Insurance designed to strengthen the traditional pension system winds up accelerating its demise.

In pursuing the objective of reducing or eliminating federal costs, policymakers have several general types of approaches available. One group consists largely of regulatory instruments, including raising premiums and adjusting them for risk, tightening the pension funding rules, improving the measurement and reporting of pension liabilities, and attempting to increase the discipline of private sponsors' funding decisions. Higher premiums – in particular, ones linked to PBGC's risk exposure – would offset losses on future claims. More accurate measurement of plans' liabilities would make the existing funding rules and premium schedule more effective.

One way to end the problem of moral hazard is to require plan sponsors to match the future pension benefit promises they make to employees by investing in high-grade bonds. If sponsors object on the grounds that the pension plan would then be too expensive, the realistic alternative is to reduce the level of promised benefits. Surely a less costly pension would be better than no pension at all.

In early 2005, the Bush Administration presented its plan for fixing the problems faced by the PBGC. A central element in this plan is fair value accounting for pension assets and liabilities. In the words of a US Treasury official speaking on behalf of the administration:[4]

> 'Some argue that the best way to enhance retirement security is to create the appearance of well funded pension plans through the use of asset and liability smoothing and increased amortization periods for actuarial losses. In addition, plan sponsors have frequently voiced their dislike of volatile and unpredictable minimum contributions. Our view is there are significant risks associated with masking the underlying financial and economic reality of underfunded pension plans. Failure to recognize risk because of the use of smoothing mechanisms results in transfers of risk among parties, in particular from plan sponsors to plan participants and the PBGC. One need only look at the losses incurred by many steel and airline plan participants and PBGC's net position to see this is so.'

The Administration has therefore proposed measuring liabilities on an accrual basis using a single standard liability measurement concept that does not distort the measures by smoothing values over time. Within the single method, liability is measured using assumptions that are appropriate for a financially healthy plan sponsor (investment grade credit rated), and alternatively using assumptions that are appropriate for a less healthy plan sponsor (below investment grade) that is more likely to find itself in a position of default on pension obligations in the short to medium term.

On-going liability is defined as the present value on the valuation date of all benefits that the sponsor is obligated to pay. Salary *projections* would not be used in determining the level of accrued benefits. Expected benefit payments would be discounted using the corporate bond spot yield curve that will be published by the Treasury Department based on market bond rates. Retirement assumptions will be developed using reasonable methodologies, based on the plan's or other relevant recent historical experience.

8.6. Conclusion

Whether or not other governments (e.g. the Netherlands) offer pension insurance as in the US and the UK, there is a strong case for government supervision based on fair value accounting. Given that the government has established incentives for private pension plans to be put in place as a matter of public policy, it is unlikely that the government could stand by and watch

---

[4]http://www.treas.gov/press/releases/reports/js2299_testimony.pdf

a significant part of the system fail. That is the political reality. Thus even in the absence of a *formal* system of pension insurance, the government is probably the *de facto* 'pension guarantor of last resort.' It should manage that responsibility without creating a misallocation of resources or unintended transfers of wealth. This goal can only be achieved on the basis of fair value accounting.

Whatever the merits of helping distressed industries through government subsidies, there are good reasons *not* to use 'cheap' pension guarantees as the way to subsidize. They are less visible to the public than other subsidies, and they can lead to serious distortions in resource allocation. If faced with a political constraint limiting the size of the premiums it can charge, the government can still adopt procedures using the other tools of management to maintain the solvency of its guarantee activity, prevent excessive risk-taking, and avoid unintended subsidies.

If it can, for instance, establish an effective system for maintaining funding standards on a mark-to-market basis, then premiums can be kept low with the system solvent. But, if it can neither charge adequate risk-based premiums nor achieve continuous full funding of insured plans, then the only route left open to the government is asset restrictions. As already discussed, even in a guarantee system that relies on risk-based premiums, some asset restrictions are required to limit moral hazard and make the guarantee contract viable.

But to rely primarily on asset restrictions (with little monitoring) to keep premiums low, the guarantor must require the insured intermediary to completely hedge its insured liabilities. If the imposition of strict matching restrictions by the government guarantor is also ruled out because it is perceived as too much government 'regulation,' then the guarantor is left with no feasible way to perform its guarantee function efficiently.

Appendix: Stocks are not a hedge against pension liabilities[5]

Many pension plan consultants and even regulators view common stocks as an asset class that matches the long-run nature of defined-benefit pension liabilities. But this belief rests on a logical fallacy.

---

[5]For a more complete development of the material in this appendix, see Zvi Bodie, 'On the Risk of Stocks in the Long Run,' *Financial Analysts Journal* May/June 1995. It has also been published as an appendix in Zvi Bodie, 'What the Pension Benefit Guaranty Corporation Can Learn from the Federal Savings and Loan Insurance Corporation,' *Journal of Financial Services Research*, Vol. 10, No. 1, January 1996.

It is important to understand why the guarantor's market-risk exposure is great even when pension fund equity portfolios are well-diversified across industry groups and consist entirely of 'blue chip' stocks. Contrary to the view that a stock portfolio is an effective hedge against the pension liability when the investment horizon is long-term, this section shows that the cost of insuring a pension liability collateralized with stocks actually *increases* with the maturity of the pension obligation.

Assume a defined-benefit plan sponsor is faced with the obligation to pay a fixed amount as a pension benefit T years from now. It fully funds its obligation by contributing to the pension fund an amount equal to the present value of the promised benefit. It can invest in an *immunized* default-free bond portfolio maturing in T years earning a certain risk-free rate of interest. If instead the sponsor invests in a stock portfolio then there is a risk of a shortfall at the maturity date.

The basis for the proposition that stocks are less risky in the long run appears to be the observation that the longer the time horizon, the smaller the *probability* of a shortfall. If the *ex ante* mean rate of return on stocks exceeds the risk-free rate of interest, it is indeed true that the probability of a shortfall declines with the length of the investment time horizon. For example, suppose the rate of return on stocks is lognormally distributed with a risk premium of 8% per year and an annualized standard deviation of 20%. With a time horizon of only one year, the probability of a shortfall is 34%, whereas at 20 years that probability is only 4%.

But the probability of a shortfall is a flawed measure of risk because it completely ignores how large the potential shortfall might be. It is easy to see this point if we assume that stock returns follow a simple 'random walk.' In any one-year period, assume the rate of return on stocks can take only one of two values C either +20 or −20%, independent of its past history. Consider the worst possible outcome for time horizons of increasing length. For a one-year horizon, one can lose 20% of the initial investment, for a two-year period 36%, and for a 20-year period as much as 99%. Using the probability of a shortfall as the measure of risk, no distinction is made between a loss of 20% or a loss of 99%.

If it were true that stocks are less risky in the long run, then the cost of insuring against earning less than the risk-free rate of interest should decline as the maturity of the pension obligation increases. But the opposite is true.

To see this, define the cost of shortfall insurance, P, as the additional amount of money one has to add at the investment starting date to assure that at the maturity date the pension portfolio will have a value at least as great as it would have, earning the risk-free interest rate. Thus, for each dollar insured against a shortfall, the total amount actually invested at the starting date is $1 + P.

To find P, we use modern option pricing methodology.[6] Insurance against shortfall risk is effectively a *put* option. The put is of the European type (i.e., it can only be exercised at the expiration date), and it matures in T years. The put's exercise price is the insured value of the portfolio. If at the expiration date T years from now the portfolio's value exceeds its insured value, then the put expires worthless. If, however, there is a shortfall, then the put's payoff is equal to the shortfall.

Because we are insuring a pension obligation that grows at the risk-free interest rate, the exercise price of the put equals the price of the underlying stock portfolio compounded at the risk-free T-year interest rate.[7] Therefore the *put-call parity theorem* tells us that the price of the put equals the price of the corresponding call.[8]

To show that the value of the put increases with T, we could use any option pricing model based on the condition that the financial markets do not allow anyone to earn risk-free arbitrage profits.[9] Because it is so compact and so widely used in practice, we will use the Black–Scholes formula. In our special case a *simplified* form of the formula can be used to compute P.

---

[6] The reference here is to the option-pricing theory originally developed by Black and Scholes (1973), and Merton (1973). There is an extensive literature on using option-pricing models to estimate the value of financial guarantees. For a comprehensive list of references, see Bodie, Zvi and R.C. Merton, 'On the Management of Financial Guarantees,' *Financial Management*, Winter 1992.

[7] Another way to state this is that the exercise price of the put equals the forward price of the underlying stock.

[8] The put-call parity theorem for European options says that: $P + S = C + Ee^{-rT}$, where P is the price of the put, S is the price of the underlying stock, C is the price of the corresponding call, E is the exercise price, and r is the risk-free interest rate. In our case: $E = Se^{rT}$. By substituting into the put-call parity relation we get: $P = C$.

[9] The option price is derived by considering a dynamic investment strategy involving only the underlying stock and the risk-free asset, which has as its objective to produce at the horizon date a payoff equal to that of the put. The strategy is self-financing, that is, no additional infusions of money beyond the original $P are required. As is well known in the literature, an option's price can also be expressed using a 'risk-neutral' valuation method. This method makes it explicit that the cost of shortfall insurance reflects a weighing of the possible shortfall magnitudes.

Figure A8.1.   Cost of shortfall insurance as a function of maturity of pension obligation

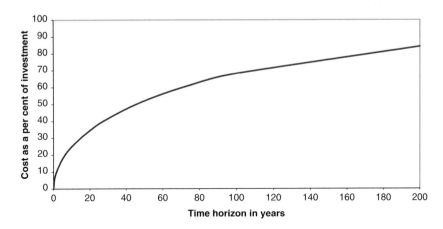

Moreover, with no loss of generality, we can express the price of the put as a fraction of the price of the stock:

$$P/S = N(d_1) - N(d_2)$$

$$d_1 = \frac{s\sqrt{T}}{2}$$

$$d_2 = \frac{-s\sqrt{T}}{2}$$

where:

S = price of the stock
T = time to maturity of the option in years
s = standard deviation of the annualized continuously compounded
        rate of return on the stock
$N(d)$ = the probability that a random draw from a standard normal
        distribution is less than d.

Note that P/S is independent of the risk-free interest rate; it depends only on s and T. Figure A8.1 shows the result of applying the formula to compute P/S assuming the annualized standard deviation of stock returns (s) is 0.2.

The cost of the insurance rises with T, the maturity of the pension obligation. For a one-year maturity, the cost is 8% of the investment. For a

10-year maturity, it is 25%, and for a 50-year maturity it is 52%. As the maturity grows without limit, the cost of the insurance approaches 100% of the investment. In other words, it can never cost more than $1 to insure that a dollar invested in stocks will earn the risk-free rate. This is because one can always invest the $1 insurance premium in risk-free bonds maturing in *T* years, so that even if the value of stocks falls to zero, the investor still will have the guaranteed minimum.

Some financial economists and other observers of the stock market have claimed that stock returns do not follow a random walk in the long run. Rather, they argue, the behavior of stock returns is best characterized as a mean-reverting process. It is mean reversion in stock returns, some say, that is the reason stocks are less risky for investors with a long time horizon. But Figure A8.1 is valid for mean-reverting processes too. The reason is that arbitrage-based option pricing models, such as the Black–Scholes or binomial models, are valid regardless of the process for the mean. They are based on the law of one price and the condition of no-arbitrage profits. Investors who disagree about the mean rate of return on stocks, but agree about the variance, will therefore agree about the option price. This is a feature of these models that may at first seem counterintuitive, but is nonetheless true.

For the relation depicted in Figure A8.1 to be invalid, mean reversion is not enough. Stock prices would have to behave just like the price of a *T*-period zero-coupon bond that converges towards the bond's face value as the horizon date approaches. In other words, stocks would have to be indistinguishable from the risk-free asset for a *T*-period horizon.

Fair Value and Pension Fund Management
N. Kortleve, T. Nijman and E. Ponds (Editors)
© 2006 Elsevier B.V.

CHAPTER 9

Value and Risk Sharing in Defined Benefit Pension Plans

Andrew Smith (Deloitte)

9.1. Introduction

In this chapter, we consider the fair value implications of pension arrangements which involve some degree of risk or cost sharing between employers and different generations of plan members. We focus particularly on the way that any value of the plan is distributed between various stakeholders.

Rather than following the numbers for a particular example, we draw out the issues involved and illustrate the typical conclusions of a fair value analysis. We focus especially on the multi-party nature of the pension plan, exploring the consequences for all stakeholders of possible plan strategies.

Our path for the remainder of the section is as follows. We start with a description of fair value analysis as applied at the plan level, focusing on the quantities commonly calculated from available modelling technologies. While fair value accounting seeks to determine a default-free value of accrued benefits to date, a full economic analysis requires an assessment of sponsor default risk and of the effect of pensions on other aspects of compensation. As these are currently not a standard part of most plans' analysis, we dwell in some detail on how these analyses may be carried out in practice.

Mechanical fair value calculations lead to the somewhat discouraging conclusion that fair value is conserved under most management strategies, so management becomes a zero sum game. We also consider risk sharing, and conclude that in a fair value world, total risk is conserved; risk management does not reduce the total risk but merely transfers risks from one party to another. The fact that risks are conserved overall does not diminish the concern of each party to understand the risks they face, for instance, these risks might be hedged outside the pension plan. We describe a methodology based on replicating portfolios which some plans have used to understand risk sharing.

In a utopian world, we would observe well functioning pension provisions, with all parties acting as in theory they should, resulting in a social optimum. However, this is not a universal pattern across Europe. Instead, the press in many countries reports pension crises, discredited actuarial theories, widening deficits, impoverished pensioners, disputes between generations over the cost of caring for the elderly, concern over inadequate private savings and failing public confidence in pension provision, amid allegations that private firms and governments exploited information asymmetries or even sought to mislead plan members. We analyse the incentives for such behaviour implied by the zero sum games. Although the pension system in some countries may be under strain, we have the dubious consolation that economic theory successfully explains the collapse we see in practice!

In the final section we explore a possible sustainable pension model. We first examine how incomplete markets provide a theoretical chink on the armour by which a modest degree of overall value creation may be possible. Clever pension plan design maximises the potential gains from co-operation. On the other hand, a comparison with other financial markets suggests that a combination of fair value disclosures and robustly enforced collateralisation reduces the potential gain from conflicts. The key to a sustainable pensions system is to ensure that each participant has more to gain from co-operation than from conflict.

9.2. Typical European pension arrangements

The range of pension arrangements in Europe is very diverse, varying both between countries and employers. However, the following features are common, particularly in the UK and Netherlands:

- A fund, invested in a mixture for bonds, equities, property and other assets.
- Insured fund management contracts in which the manager may also provide various forms of capital guarantees or smoothing of returns over time.
- Minimum guaranteed benefits taking the form of annuities for retiring members, with the initial annuity amount depending on a member's time or service and salary history.

- Arrangements for members leaving the plan when they leave employment before retirement. This may be in the form of a lump sum transfer value to another pension arrangement, or as a deferred benefit, that is, a pension whose annual value is fixed now but which can only be drawn from normal retirement age.
- Significant employer discretion to provide more generous benefits, including benefit increases in retirement or deferment or special early retirement arrangements, and usually contingent on the health of the fund.
- Regular actuarial valuations of assets and liabilities on a variety of calculation bases, producing statements that the plan is in surplus or in deficit.
- Variable contributions from both members and employees. The employer contributions are often calculated by reference to the valuation surplus or deficits, so that, contributions may be increased so that, under certain assumptions, a valuation deficit is eliminated over, for example, a 10 year period.

Each of these features gives rise to particular complexities in the analysis of a pension deal. We propose to analyse pension plans using projections of the cash flows which the plans generate – in order to understand better how values and risks are shared between plan participants, and to explain the incentives faced by the many parties involved. To capture many important plan features, it is often necessary to project cash flows stochastically, with associated probabilities and processes for market-consistent valuation. These methods are described in more detail in the paper by Exley and Hibbert.

A fair value analysis requires realistic estimates of the market value of these cash flows. This means that all material aspects of the cash flows should be modelled, including the way in which the fund manager smooths investment returns, the calculation of plan contributions and the operation of any sponsor discretion. The projection of these cash flows may also require the future simulation of calculations which affect cash flows, such as asset turnover assumptions for projecting historic cost asset valuations (where these affect cash flows), and the application of actuarial assumptions to drive actuarial liability valuations. Even when some other accounting basis forms the basis for determining contributions or investments, or even disclosed financial statements, the fair value is still useful for the management of the plan.

9.3. Stakeholders and fair value stakes – the plan centred analysis

The performance of a pension plan can affect many parties. We will consider a range of models, starting from simple plan-centric models and then moving on to models that include other parties including their members and corporate sponsors.

The simplest possible plan model involves only the direct stakeholders in the plan, that is:

- The members, who receive benefits, and may make contributions. The population of members may be split in several ways, for example, between active, deferred and retired members, or between different dates of past entry to the plan.
- The corporate sponsor, who pays contributions into the fund.
- The fund manager who buys and sells assets, passing on smoothed investment return net of fees and making up any returns below the guaranteed minimum. The smoothing may take a number of forms, including explicit moving average smoothing, the withholding of good investment returns for later use in discretionary benefit payments, or the use of book value accounting.
- An expense sink, that is, an artificial construction that exists to receive expenses, taxes and other miscellaneous cash flows.

An analysis of the direct stakeholders is sometimes called a *plan-centric* analysis. Such an analysis chooses a fixed time window, and examines the projected cash flows from the date of the investigation until the end of the fixed time window. The analysed cash flows might include:

- Contributions into the fund, from both sponsor and employers
- Pension benefits paid from the fund to plan members
- Cash flows used to buy or sell participations in the fund
- Other expenses, fund management fees and taxes

In this simple model we do not allow the plan to accumulate any cash of its own. All cash flowing into the fund is instantly invested with the fund manager and all cash flowing out of the fund is obtained by asset sales. In this case, the net cash flow in any period is zero.

Analysts can compute the fair value of each of these streams of cash flows, using the discount factors in the chosen stochastic model. We can define the fair value of each stakeholder's stake in the fund as follows:

- The fair value of the members' stake is the fair value of benefits minus the value of the fair value of member contributions.
- The fair value of the sponsor's stake is the fair value of employers' contributions, with a negative sign.
- The fair value of the fund manager's stake is the fair value of the 'purchase' cash flows minus the 'sale' cash flows.
- The fair value of the expense sink is the fair value of expenses, taxes or other miscellaneous costs not modelled elsewhere.

The fair value stakes do not usually equate to other accounting measures. Accounting measures of assets may relate to fair values or historic costs. Even where an accounting measure is claimed to represent fair valuation, this may in practice be compromised by other concessions. For example, accounting measures of liabilities may exclude the impact of discretionary behaviour, and may also require the use of above risk-free assumptions for interest rates. Accounting measures seldom require the stochastic projections of cash flows which are usually necessary for a fair value assessment.

The use of fair values is particularly illuminating in respect of the fund managers' stake. Let us assume for the moment that there are no underlying guarantees, no return smoothing and no fund manager fees. In this case, the value of future purchases will be offset by the eventual sale of those same assets, and the fair value of the fund manager's stake is a liability equal to the fair value of the assets already in the fund. As the fund manager also has those assets, his net position is zero. At first sight, this is discouraging, because it suggests that whatever the asset strategy adopted, the fund manager can add no value. On closer inspection, we see that this finding is a consequence of the use of fair values calibrated to market prices. As our fair valuation model replicates market prices of all assets, then by definition, no asset is mispriced.

Allowing for the complexity of real fund management contracts, the fund manager's liability is reduced to the extent of any management charges, but increased by the cost of any guarantees or smoothing. In some countries, the fund manager or associated insurer provides implicit or explicit guarantees, including guarantees of entry and exit from the fund on fixed terms. In that case, the fund manager (or her own shareholders) becomes important players and risk bearers in the pension system.

164 A. Smith

In our fund manager thought experiment, we have implicitly projected all cash flows forever, and obtained an infinite horizon fair value. However, this approach is difficult to compute in practice. The difficulty arises because the cash flows are valued by simulation, and the more distant cash flows are subject to greater variability. This variability introduces sampling error to the estimation of fair values, because we are taking the average of random simulations. The sampling error can be reduced by running a larger number of random simulations. However many simulations are run, the sampling error is relatively larger for longer dated cash flows. There comes a time horizon beyond which further projections contribute little additional information.

For this reason, analysts will often project the difficult cash flows (such as the operation of discretion, profit sharing or complicated contribution rules) only to a fairly short fixed time horizon, such as ten years, and construct a 'proxy' valuation for the cash flows beyond that point in time, using closed form solutions based on the prevailing interest rates at the end of the ten years. For example, when valuing the pension liability cash flows, the actual cash flows might be projected for the next ten years, while the value of all future cash flows may be assumed to be captured by an actuarial valuation in ten years' time. If the actuarial valuation is close to a market basis for the cash flows beyond the horizon, then this proxy method can produce good estimates of fair values for the infinite cash flow stream.

Even with this simple model, it is possible to draw some general conclusions about the operation of typical pension plans, with regard to funding policy and investment strategy.

The impact of funding strategy is clear. A better funded plan is better for current and future members who are more likely to benefit from discretionary improvements, and may also benefit from lower member contributions. This gain is at the expense of today's contributors. Although a large sponsor contribution now reduces the expected contributions required in future, there is an overall sponsor loss because some of today's contribution leaks out to members in the form of discretionary benefits. See the paper of Kortleve and Ponds (*this volume*) for further explanations of this effect.

A risky investment strategy will benefit members who receive from discretionary benefits in the event of good performance but are insulated from poor returns by the minimum benefit guarantee. In the absence of fund manager guarantees, this benefit is often at the expense of the corporate sponsor, particularly if the sponsor is solely responsible for making up contribution shortfalls. The situation is less clear cut where the fund manager offers smoothing and return guarantees. It may at first sight seem that the sponsor can off-load the guarantee costs onto the fund manager by selecting guaranteed funds. However, wise fund managers, controlling risky assets, recognise the higher value of guarantees and devise charging structures to generate higher annual fees.

A notable feature of this analysis is the 'zero sum game'. As cash flows sum to zero, so too must the fair values. The fair value analysis contrasts with traditional actuarial thinking, which has sometimes argued that the higher returns on risky assets can be shared among the plan stakeholders while the risk evaporates if you wait long enough.

It is important to understand why this zero sum game arises. Building the scenario generation and other projection assumptions requires modellers to take a view on many aspects for which no direct market price can be observed – for example, salary progressions, actuarial decrements or correlations between different risk factors. The easiest route – and therefore the one most often taken – is to use the same set of simulations, and so the same non-market view – when evaluating the stakes of each stakeholder. In that case, sampling error aside, the zero sum game is sure to emerge from the analysis.

9.4. Extending the model to allow credit risk

The plan-centric model allows a simple assessment of cash flows, but ignores many important financial aspects of the plan, especially in situations of very poor returns. If the plan, or the sponsor, becomes insolvent then a new set of rules take over. Plan members usually enjoy a charge over the plan assets, but order of priority rules usually favour some classes of members (for example, pensioners) over others. Various rules apply when a plan is wound up, which vary from country to country and according to the legal framework under which the plan was first put together. In most countries, members of insolvent plans join a long line of creditors who may share in some way in the assets of the sponsor.

It is plain that our simple plan-centric model cannot capture these subtleties, because we have not yet modelled the corporation. Ideally, we would like to model the interaction between the plan on the sponsor's business, including the effect of the plan on the sponsor's financial strength and, conversely, any member credit risk to the plan arising from future sponsor failure. More broadly, we can even consider the effect of a pension plan on the likely sponsor share price.

Fortunately, a great deal is known about corporate valuations. We know how to construct corporate valuations from discounted dividends, or, equivalently, from discounted profits minus the cost of capital. The debt market also tells us a lot about how the market values the risk of corporate default. A growing number of companies are extending their pension valuation models to include some measure of their own default risk.

The calibration of credit risk is not always straightforward. Many economic scenario generators are goods at replicating market prices for the most liquid options, those protecting against likely moves in equities or interest rates. Option prices are more difficult to obtain for extreme strike prices. A stochastic model calibrated to option prices may imply a price for corporate credit risk, but the implied spread is often several times smaller than that actually seen on corporate bonds. Reasons for the differences include a failure of many standard models to replicate tail behaviour, and the failure of many cash flow models to anticipate all possible adverse events which could lead to default.

The effect of investment strategy is now more subtle when credit risk is taken into account. In the absence of fund manager guarantees, some of the risk of poor returns passes onto the plan members. This is because poor investment returns may also be associated with poor trading conditions for the sponsor, resulting in sponsor default on contributions at the same time as the fund is in deficit. Where the fund manager does offer guaranteed returns, some of this credit risk still remains, as poor market returns impose guarantee costs on fund managers, who in turn are more likely to fail under this burden. The effect on plan members depends on the details of the fund management contract and the operation of any fund segregation.

The effect of funding strategy is much clearer, at least where all contributions come from the sponsor. A cash injection to a pension plan from a sponsor improves the credit position of plan members, at a cost to the sponsor. This combines with the effect of discretionary pension increases to create a world where members wish sponsors to keep a plan well funded but sponsors are reluctant to comply.

The effect of credit risk may be distributed unevenly across different classes of members. For example, in situations of a plan wind-up, it may be possible to buy annuities from a third party, for example an insurance company. An annuity buy-out strategy immediately pushes existing pensioners to the front of the line of plan creditors. The cash outflow required to buy the annuities may further weaken the plan, which may have the greatest impact on those near to retirement, because these members have the largest sums at risk of default. Therefore, we can expect different plan members to have divergent views on the wisdom or otherwise of risk taking within a pension plan.

Within our zero sum game framework, the cost of credit risk borne by members must show up as a gain elsewhere in the system. At first sight, the winner seems to be the sponsoring company, who is then spared the burden of future contributions and, in some situations can invoke limited liability to walk away from a plan in deficit.

More extensive models can further trace the costs and benefits of corporate failures. It seems odd, with hindsight, to argue that shareholders have benefited in the event that their investment becomes worthless. It also seems odd that shareholders would sanction risky asset strategies which threaten their core investment. This line of thought leads us to investigate the core business of the sponsor – which is not usually the operation of a pension plan, but the manufacture of goods and services in an entirely different industry. If a company enjoys a competitive advantage in its core industry, then its value derives from the ability to sell a product for more than its manufacture cost. Shareholders are unlikely to allow a pension fund deficit to trigger company insolvency. More likely, if the underlying business is profitable, managers will arrange refinancing. In this case, default is avoided.

When default does occur, a purely mathematical analysis therefore suggests that the winners in the event of company failure would be the suppliers and customers. In a fair value world, these groups of people would theoretically gain when an intermediary's profit margin is eliminated from the system. The extent to which these gains accrue to each party depends on model assumptions about the 'fair' value of goods supplied relative to the price actually paid. Economically, however, this provides little insight, saying us more about the limitations of the cash flow model than it does about corporate finance. If the eliminated point of the chain had a competitive efficiency advantage, then it is likely to be replaced by a less efficient competitor, who then becomes the primary beneficiary of the original plan sponsor's demise. In addition, we should not overlook the substantial costs of liquidation, which represent costs to shareholders or bondholders and gains to administrators, lawyers or even actuaries.

9.5. Pensions in the context of employment compensation

From a labour economics perspective, it is natural to ask whether a pension plan is a cost-effective tool for employee compensation. This requires a more detailed assessment of the relationship between the sponsor and employees, and in particular an assessment of any credit the employees may give for the pension plan in salary negotiations. These aspects are important, because much advice on pensions matters is, at least theoretically, directed at plan members or their representatives. An assessment of member impact should include all consequences of a pension change.

Labour economics leads to a further extension of the network of cash flows captured by a pension model. The labour contract involves an exchange of labour for compensation. The compensation includes a main salary, and also any pension benefits in excess of member contributions. There may also be other benefits such as company cars or health insurance, which for current purposes we treat as part of the main salary.

Despite the large variations in pension plan design, we can still draw some general conclusions about the key drivers of member value. The first key decision is how to model the salary bargaining process. For example, let us suppose that main salary is unaffected by pension arrangements, and that sponsor credit risk is minimal. In that case, a move to a more conservative investment strategy reduces the scope for discretionary benefits. As we have already discussed, this represents a gain for the plan sponsor and a loss for members. This could be an accurate description of the situation when members place a low value on pension promises – either because of credit risk concerns or because (in some countries) generous pension benefits simply reduce the state benefits to which a pensioner would otherwise be entitled. In that case, sponsors may be able to erode promised benefits steadily without facing higher main salary costs.

However, if the labour market adjusts to market levels of total compensation, different dynamics come into play. In the event that the sponsor reduces the value of pension benefits, they may simply have to pay more to recruit and retain staff. In this case, the reduction in pension benefits simply represents a rearrangement of the pay package from deferred to current compensation. In fair value terms there is no effect at all – and in particular, the sponsor saves nothing by cutting back benefits.

The labour market analysis becomes more complex when we consider corporate failure. A simple model would consider only the cash flows to members – that is, salary and pension benefits. Corporate failure then appears to impose a huge cost on the workforce. However, such an analysis overstates the impact, because it ignores the possibility that some workers will replace their salary elsewhere – and may even be entitled to redundancy or early retirement provisions which leave them better off than they were before.

The early-leaver benefits and order of priority become important in under-standing winners and losers in these situations. Even those workers who do not immediately find new employment may nevertheless be entitled to state benefits, and are also spared some of the expenses, such as travel and childcare costs, associated with being employed.

Therefore, to model the effect of a pension plan on members, we should consider not only the benefits they currently receive, but also the benefits they could receive in alternative employment. The member loss on spon-sor default is the difference between these two numbers and not the gross employment cost.

9.6. Quantifying the sharing of risk using replicating portfolios

The fair value approach gives us tools for the valuation of future cash flows. It enables us to see how future cash flow streams redistribute value between participants.

We can also use fair value tools to understand better how risks are shared between stakeholders. The relevant construction is that of a 'replicating portfolio'.

The replicating portfolio is useful because it enables different parties to understand the risks to which they are exposed. For example, the fund manager may construct a replicating portfolio for his own liabilities, based on expected cash flows and the operation of any smoothing or guarantees. It is frequently the case that the replicating portfolio involves lower risk assets compared to the actual assets held. The fund manager then bears the mismatch risk between her own assets and liabilities. She may wish to adjust the asset mix held, or to hold offsetting positions outside the pension plan assets, in order to manage that risk.

In the same way, the corporate sponsor may examine the replicating portfolio for their contributions to the plan. Many sponsors already use value-at-risk or similar tools for their own corporate risk management purposes. A plan sponsor might decide to allocate equity capital outside the pension plan to provide a cushion against the risk that adverse pension develop-ments cause the company to fail. Alternatively, the sponsor may seek to hedge the resulting risk exposures alongside other market risks within the corporate treasury function. Pensions may hitherto have been excluded from these analyses, either on grounds of complexity or on the questionable grounds that short-term monitoring is inappropriate for short term risks.

The construction of replicating portfolios substantially removes these obstacles to the integration of pension plans into a corporate risk framework.

Replicating portfolios also enable plan members to see the risks to which they are exposed in a pension plan. Some employees may have additional alternative savings vehicles, such as direct investment in bond or stock market funds. Members may be interested to compare the compulsory economic exposures they gain from the pension plan, to the economic risks which the member might have chosen given a free hand. For example, when benefits reflect smoothed investment returns or discretionary participation in surpluses, the replicating portfolio may include alternating large long and short positions in zero coupon bonds over a range of terms. Classical theories of portfolio selection would be unlikely to identify such portfolios as an optimal choice from a member perspective. Members furnished with replicating portfolio may even adjust other personal assets in order to offset exposures gained via a pension plan. For example, if the corporate pension plan gives a member a lower exposure to the equity market than they would choose, the member may re-allocate other assets outside the pension plan to stock market investments.

A replicating portfolio of assets is defined as a portfolio with the same value as a stakeholder's stake. This equality is preserved not only under current market conditions, but also under selected market moves.

In a perfect world, our economic scenario generator would model stochastically all the separate risk factors to which plan participants are exposed. However, this yields unnecessarily cumbersome models. For example, in principle every separate point on the yield curve could be its own factor, but many useful models treat the yield curve with only one or two factors. To take another example, models based on normal distributions often produce deterministic option implied volatilities, while traded option markets reveal constantly fluctuating option implied volatilities.

Exley and Hibbert (*this volume*) refer to replicating portfolios within the framework of an assumed model or scenario generator. In theory, these can replicate perfectly if the model assumptions hold and the replicating portfolio is rebalanced continuously and without costs. However, when this replication is modelled over time, the replication may in fact be poor, because of additional factors not modelled stochastically within the scenario generator.

It turns out that replication effectiveness can be improved dramatically by the use of stress tests. This allows the extension of the replicating portfolio to cover additional effects, such as changing volatilities or odd shaped yield chiefs, not captured by the underlying scenario generator. Such a replicating portfolio construction requires the following choices:

- A list of basis replicating assets, usually including cash, bonds of various terms, equities, property and possibly also including derivatives such as equity options and swaptions. These will be combined in suitable proportions to produce the replicating portfolios.
- A list of stress tests to be applied to both basis replicating assets and cash flow valuations.

The stress tests should correspond to the list of possible replicating assets. For example, if the replicating asset list includes bonds of five different terms, appropriate stress tests could stress five different segments of the forward yield curve. If the replicating assets include swaptions of three different terms then three stress tests to the interest rate volatility surface would be necessary. The number of base replicating assets (including cash) should equal the number of stress tests (including the base case under current market conditions), both of which may be far large than the number of stochastic factors actually captured stochastically in the scenario generator. It is also necessary to avoid linear dependence between basis replicating assets. For example, if zero coupon bonds of all terms are included in the basis assets, it would not be appropriate also to include forward rate agreements or interest rate swaps, as these can be synthesised from zero coupon bonds and so any replicating portfolio would not be unique.

The next step in the replicating portfolio construction is to revalue both assets and liabilities under the stress scenarios. The replicating portfolio for a set of cash flows is determined by a series of linear equations, one for each basis replicating asset, or equivalently, one for each stress test. Each stress test needs an accompanying set of simulations from a random scenario generator, so the number of possible stress tests may be limited by the flexibility of the scenario generator calibration process.

The resulting replicating portfolios are generally robust to changes in the specification of the stress tests – for example whether the yield curve shocks are upwards or downwards. This robustness works provided that the cash flow fair values (and base asset fair values) are approximately linear in the parameters underlying the asset model.

Care is required over the number of simulations required. Asset and cash flow values may be misstated because of sampling error in the simulations, although there may be substantial cancellations if assets and liabilities are closely matched. In the mismatched case, the sampling error can propagate through the system of linear equations, resulting in unstable replicating portfolios. The main remedy against such propagation is to use the same set of simulations for assets and cash flow valuation. Some scenario generators allow recalibrations to be implemented as a modification to an existing scenario set rather than as a new independent set of simulations. This is desirable because it ensures that any cash flow value changes in a stress test are genuinely due to the stress test itself and not to randomness in the simulations.

Replicating portfolios satisfy the same zero-sum-game constraints as cash flow fair values. If we add the replicating portfolios for all parties we must come back to the underlying asset portfolio for the plan. If there is an underlying investment in property, then someone must bear that risk. In a fair value world, the application of smoothing cannot eliminate risk, but simply passes it from one party to another.

The replicating portfolio construction copes well with market risks, but is less informative in relation to risks such as increases in longevity, that is, reductions in mortality rates. The lack of market prices for these risks means that assumptions need to be made about how such instruments would theoretically be priced. Nevertheless, the underlying conservation rules still apply. If improving longevity makes old people expensive to look after, you cannot make it any cheaper by clever risk sharing, but you can affect who is exposed to that risk.

9.7. The bargaining problem

Most pension plans have been designed with a stated aim of providing secure and generous benefits at modest cost. Much of pensions advice revolves around an optimisation process which aims to minimise risk subject to acceptable returns. It may seem obvious that such a low-risk, high-return strategy would benefit most of the stakeholders, if such a strategy existed. Actuaries may attempt to act as honest brokers, finding an optimal solution which works for everybody.

The fair value model instead suggests a bargaining game, where there are no common gains to seek, and every player's gain is at someone else's expense. Edgeworth first proposed this problem in 1881. Two impatient players repeatedly make offers on the sharing of a cake, and the game ends when one party finally accepts an offer made by the other side.

The difficulty is in predicting where such a game ends up. Edgeworth argued that, without competition, the solution was indeterminate; there is no way of predicting what bargain might be struck. Over the next 70 years many other great economists, including John Hicks and Alfred Marshall, took up this problem but made no headway. The first substantial progress on this problem came from John Nash (1950) who applied game theoretical tools.

Subsequent work on the bargaining problem has focused on the negotiation skills and any other leverage which either party might bring to bear in the negotiating process. Game theory still yields no unique fair solution to the bargaining problem.

This is illuminating from the perspective of a pension plan. In the absence of common benefits, most decisions reduce to bargaining games. For example, a fair value analysis offers no optimal investment strategy or funding strategy for pension plans. The observed degree of funding seen in plans may be better explained by an examination of the negotiating power of employers, members, regulators, fund managers, advisors and other stakeholders. Where members have the upper hand in negotiations, strongly funded plans will result. When sponsors control funding policy, slower funding would be the likely outcome.

The lack of a consensus equilibrium emphasises the need for a fair valuation of pension cash flows. Each stakeholder should carefully monitor the fair value of their stake, sure in the knowledge that any deal reached behind closed doors will be damaging to those not represented.

In this bargaining game, there may still be a major role for classical risk-return analysis, albeit a more sinister one. For example, in the UK such risk-return analysis (going under the name of ALM) has been used to justify heavy investment in equities, which also (at the time) was accompanied by favourable accounting treatment and lower required contributions. Corporate sponsors may well desire the benefits of flexible accounting and lower contributions. However, an open declaration of that intent could alert analysts and employee representatives. Sponsors may well have found it more effective to achieve their objectives quietly, under cover of an expert ALM report. This is an example of an information asymmetry, which we now move on to consider.

9.8. Information asymmetries and the gridlock solution

Our analysis so far has assumed that all parties have equal access to information and equal abilities to process that information. We now consider the chief information asymmetries and the likely consequences of these for pension provision. We also explore the practice of collateralised trading in capital markets, which has many similarities to pensions but is simpler because of the lack of information asymmetries.

The most obvious information asymmetry relates to sponsors and plan members. In many countries, corporate sponsors can commission detailed analysis of their pension arrangements, including analysis of many aspects of risks and returns. Members do not necessarily have access to this information, or the power to commission investigations from their own point of view. Despite the efforts of accounting standard setters, few pension plans report their liability fair values externally.

With the exception of derivative dealers, management at most firms using derivatives also oppose fair value financial reporting. The reasons given are different, with pension managers complaining of 'short term volatility' on a long term commitment, while corporations focus on 'hedge accounting' which means that non-fair-value treatment of underlying lending or borrowing arrangements is extended to derivatives. Whatever the underlying rationale, the consequence is the same – that potentially useful fair value information is withheld from users of financial statements. These give rise to important information asymmetries.

Even if members can access numbers they may not be able to interpret them to take sensible decisions. Information about possible default is particularly difficult to obtain.

The information asymmetry generates a 'gridlock' Nash equilibrium of mutual distrust where:

- The sponsor has an incentive to maximise credit risk if members are unable to measure this.
- Members will naturally assume that the sponsor follows the financial incentive, and value the benefits accordingly.
- The sponsor therefore has to maximise credit risk, as the value-destroying alternative is to offer benefits that are more valuable than the members will recognise.

Another well-documented information asymmetry affects shareholders and managers of a business. Pensions are complex, and financial reporting will always be difficult. Even the best drafted financial reporting standard will overlook some subtleties in benefit structures. As a result there is a risk that corporate managers can:

- Grant subtle improvements in pension benefits
- For which members will accept more modest salaries
- Disclosing financial results which show reduced operating costs (because the pension burden is understated)
- And therefore claiming performance related bonuses for themselves

This is a classic example of 'agency effects'. The agency effect also gives rise to a gridlock Nash equilibrium, where financial statements are less than candid and so mistrusted by capital providers. In this case, we have the additional complication that the fund may need to maintain a risky asset strategy purely in order to sustain the low accounting value for liability.

The gridlock equilibriums are discouraging, because they suggests that well funded, well run, pension plans may not be sustainable. Instead, every party maximises their wealth by trying to extract the wealth of others, often with less than transparent disclosure.

9.9. Public and private valuations and the incomplete markets problem

The zero sum game and gridlock analysis relied heavily on our use of the same model to value all stakes. Incomplete markets provide the possibility of super-additive valuations, where, in respect of non-market risks, all parties can gain from a transaction.

The fair value of a traded asset is unambiguously its market value. The fair value of a pension cash flow is less well defined. It depends somewhat awkwardly on modelling assumptions. Examples of critical model assumptions include:

- Progressions of salaries
- Exercise of discretion in smoothing of returns, investment strategy, funding calculations and benefit improvements
- Mortality and other actuarial decrements
- Risks affecting the profitability and security of the core business
- The definition of total returns for assets taxed differently in the hands of different investors. This is particularly problematic for equities, where some investors will be taxed on dividend income while others may receive a dividend tax credit which may be used elsewhere.

- Correlations, particularly between the performance of fund asset and the sponsor's core business

Economists speak of 'complete' markets, in which traded assets would imply market prices for all these risks. In a hypothetical complete market, all these risks could be hedged at a market price and there would be no room for disagreement on the correct prices.

The valuations arising from a calibrated scenario generator will attach prices to these risks for which no market price is observable. Consciously or unconsciously, the designer of the scenario generator must form a view on where a theoretically correct market price should lie. Some theoretical tools exist to link market prices to statistical time series behaviour, but there remains freedom for different analysts to take different views. This means that, while fair values are constrained to some degree by market prices, greater freedom exists for risks not priced by the market.

The lack of complete markets also means that investors can maintain different private valuations. For example, some authors suggest that individuals may exhibit 'habit formation'. This gives rise to mathematically complex utility functions which harshly penalise scenarios where consumption falls from one period to the next. Furthermore, habit formation relates utility to changes in main salary, which is one of the major risks for which we lack market prices. A habit formation model would attach a particularly high utility to pension benefits which relate to previous salary, as it mitigates the risk of a sharp fall in consumption at the point of retirement.

The corporation may view the pension salary link differently, particularly if the pensions are linked to a payroll figure over which the sponsor exercises some control. In a complete market, members might buy salary-linked bonds from corporate sponsors, and the existence of a market would cause a market-wide convergence on the cost of salary risk. In the incomplete market, a pension plan may provide a vehicle which achieves a similar effect but without the price transparency or convergence. This is perhaps our best hope of breaking out of the zero-sum game, and devising pension solutions which can truly benefit all parties. If the gains from different valuations in incomplete markets are large enough, then parties to a pension deal may conclude they have more to gain from cooperation than conflict.

There are other effects which work in the opposite direction. Too often, a pension plan forces members to take a large part of their compensation in the form of an opaque and illiquid pension asset. The credit risk for this asset is poorly diversified, and strongly correlated with the member's timely receipt of main salary. Members may privately discount the asset value for these undesirable aspects, but neither of these discounts results in a corresponding saving for the other parties. We then have a potential example of a negative sum game, where sponsor's cost of providing pension benefits exceeds the value which members place on those benefits. This analysis suggests that the mitigation of credit risk is fundamental to the development of a sustainable pensions model. We now consider the most successful tool for credit risk outside the pensions world, that is, collateralisation.

9.10. Collateralisation

The game theoretical analysis has the somewhat disappointing conclusion that there is no right way to fund a pension plan. Instead, the outcome will be a negotiated process. However, the bargaining problem applies not only to pension plans but to any transaction involving credit risk on deferred promises. Outside the pensions area, the funding concept is called 'collateralisation' and we see a much greater degree of consensus.

Collateralised trading, or margining, is almost universal in financial markets. Two parties agree on a financial transaction. The transaction is revalued daily on a fair value wind-up basis. Whichever party has a liability (the debtor) will provide liquid collateral, usually cash or bonds, either directly to the other party (the creditor) or to a third party who holds the assets in trust. These collateral payments are updated daily, via a process called margining. If the debtor fails to honour increasing collateral requirements, or the creditor fails to refund collateral on a decrease, the deal is immediately void and the collateral passes from the debtor to the creditor. As the collateral is assessed on a fair value basis, the creditor can use the collateral to restart the deal with another party.

As the paper of Foley (*this volume*) points out, the process of margining does not eliminate credit risk, but it is substantially reduced. The most either party can lose is one day's movement in collateral plus the transaction costs of restarting the deal with a third party. This is a very substantial improvement on the non-collateralised situation where the whole value of the transaction is at risk of credit default.

The following financial markets make extensive use of collateralised trading to reduce credit risk:

– Exchange traded derivatives
– Over-the-counter derivatives

– Equity and bond repurchase markets
– Asset and liability securitisations
– Other secured lending

Funding a pension plan is another example of collateralisation. In the event of sponsor failure, the members usually gain control of the underlying assets. The surplus or deficit in a pension fund corresponds to the collateral movement in a margined trade. This provides some protection to members in the event of default. However, there are also some obvious differences:

• Pension funding is usually not on a fair value basis. Even the assets may not necessarily be evaluated at market value.
• Pension valuations may be performed annually or even less frequently instead of every day.
• Deficits or surpluses are remedied over a period of years rather than the same day.
• Pension valuations often involve projections of future decrements, salary increases and other variables while margining calculations are usually on an immediate wind-up basis.
• Pension managers pay a great deal of attention to the investment strategy of the fund, with regard especially to long term returns. In contrast, the main focus of collateral asset selection is liquidity.
• As a consequence of these differences, wound up pension funds may end up with an asset portfolio which is less than half the liability fair value, and which is difficult to realise because of liquidity problems.

It is hard to escape the conclusion that pension plans, if they wished, could reduce the credit exposure substantially by learning lessons from the collateralisation business.

9.11. The sustainable Nash equilibrium

Thankfully, gridlock is not the only Nash equilibrium. Instead, we can introduce a possible role for a new class of professionals who certify the integrity of a pension plan, therefore easing the information asymmetry.

• The sponsor keeps the fund well-funded, and this is independently certified by a qualified professional. The sponsor now lacks the incentive to increase credit risk as this would result in withdrawal of certification.

- The profession recognises that its existence depends on strictly policed standards, so acts decisively to enforce funding certification standards.
- Members have confidence in the funding certification and therefore recognise the strong pension fund as a valuable part of the compensation package.

We still lack some of the ingredients of a cooperative equilibrium, because the professionals themselves may face difficult incentives. Given that the funding problem is a bargaining game rather than a competitive equilibrium, the lack of consensus view is unsurprising. The instability arises because certifiers whose liability valuations are at the lower end of the justifiable range can gain a competitive advantage in the certification market – a phenomenon known as 'competition in laxity'. The more conservative certifiers have an invidious choice of:

- Abandoning their principles and reducing liability valuations
- Exiting the market, and losing their influence of standard setting
- Trying to develop a distinctive brand for sound valuations – a message which at best falls on deaf ears because of information asymmetries and at worst simply discredits the whole profession

In this section, we have assumed that the sponsor retains the upper hand in the appointment of certifiers. We could consider an alternative model in which member representatives, for example trade, unions, were selecting advisors. In this case, the same element of competition could act in reverse, resulting in increasing liability valuations, large contributions and ultimately, large hidden surpluses in pension plans.

The use of fair values substantially mitigates these instabilities and can break the gridlock. While a certifier may be tempted, for example, to argue for the use of expected equity returns to discount fixed liabilities, a well run professional body could quickly terminate such abuse by testing against fair value principles, and learning lessons from the success of collateralisation elsewhere in the financial system.

9.12. Conclusion

Fair value techniques are causing a quiet revolution in the way pension plans are managed and reported.

In the short term, fair value techniques are widely misunderstood. Users fear that fair values will result in volatile results, management will lose control of financial statements, plan members will panic at the size of disclosed fair value deficits, and that proposed changes in management strategy will face an impossibly high hurdle of proving universal gains for everybody.

However, the lack of fair value reporting also creates information asymmetries between plan members, corporate managers and shareholders. The information asymmetries lead to gridlock equilibriums where accounting information is justifiability discounted because managers exploit all loopholes to the maximum degree.

A move to fair value resolves many of the information asymmetries. As more corporations examine fair values, their understanding of the financial issues also improves. The forthcoming changes are less frightening than they first appeared.

Fair Value and Pension Fund Management
N. Kortleve, T. Nijman and E. Ponds (Editors)

CHAPTER 10

Pension Deals and Value-Based ALM

Niels Kortleve (PGGM)[a,1] and Eduard Ponds (ABP and Netspar)[b,1]

Abstract

High expected returns for equities do not imply that equities are more attractive. Value-based ALM shows that poor equity returns come in economic bad times and that raising contributions and/or lowering benefits (cutting nominal benefits or cutting indexation) is very expensive in these circumstances. Equities will often outperform the riskless asset and on average result in cheaper funding and higher benefits, but this is offset by poor times, often even more than offset! Value-based ALM leads to the insight that current stakeholders often lose by taking more risk in the form of investing in equities. Next to that, investing in equities increases the size of 'option surplus' and 'option deficit,' the present value of future surpluses and deficits. Thereby the risk will increase and the sustainability of the pension deal decreases since the future outcome can be very unattractive for one group of stakeholders.

We will use the new approach of value-based ALM to investigate pension deals ranging from pure defined benefit to pure defined contribution and to asset allocations of 100% in equities versus 100% in bonds. We will show that seemingly attractive pension deals, that have for instance low average contribution rates and high expected surpluses, may have low present values for certain stakeholders. Value-based ALM will show who will gain and loose from changing the current pension deal. This information in our opinion will help to construct a more sustainable pension deal.

---

[a]Niels Kortleve is a manager Actuarial Projects & Special Accounts for PGGM; [b]Eduard Ponds is head of strategy, Financial and Risk Policy Department, ABP and senior researcher for Netspar.
[1]We are very grateful to Theo Nijman for his comments, Elbert Schrier and Jeroen Trip for their support in generating the results.

Value-based ALM adds new information relative to classical ALM in the form of present values of future cash flows, the economic value of future surpluses and deficits as well as stakeholder information, showing the intergenerational solidarity expressed in economic value terms. We think this information should no longer be disregarded and should be included in doing ALM and constructing pension deals in the future.

JEL codes: G13, G23, H55 and M41

10.1. Introduction

In the pension industry, Asset Liability Management (ALM) is being used to come to optimal pension deals. Board members of pension plans have to decide what the optimal funding strategy, indexation policy and investment strategy is for the fund, as well as how risks best can be shared over the various stakeholders like members and sponsor. ALM outcomes could suggest to increase contributions in periods of poor investment returns – and for Defined Benefit plans low funding ratios – and to lower indexation or even cut benefits (in the case of Defined Contribution). Within ALM, one looks to the possible distributions amongst others contributions, indexation and funding ratio to form an opinion on the attractiveness of the strategy being considered.

Value-based ALM adds an extra, new dimension by showing the present value – also called economic value – of all decisions about the funding strategy, indexation policy and investment strategy. Using the techniques described in the previous chapters,[2] one can calculate the present value of contributions (conditional), benefits (including indexation) and shortfalls/surpluses for the fund collectively and also for the various stakeholders. This addition leads to at least two types of extra insights, which we will discuss in more detail in Section 10.2. The main conclusions are that economic value will lead to different insights in the attractiveness and sustainability of a pension deal for the pension fund and for its stakeholders.

---

[2]See chapters of Hibbert *et al.* (2006) and Nijman and Koijen (2006) for technique and Exley (2006) for concepts.

Value-based ALM could thus lead to even better pension deals and risk sharing within pension plans.

An extra reason for applying value-based ALM is the broad shift to fair value that one can notice in (international) accounting standards and in supervision of pension funds and insurance companies.[3] Fair value does not only give relevant information for shareholders, but also for other stakeholders like members and leads to more transparent and easier to understand information about the pension deal. Supervisors are working on frameworks incorporating fair value for both assets and liabilities, making value-based ALM an even more sensible approach.

10.2. Characteristics of value-based ALM

What are the main characteristics of a value-based ALM approach for strategic decision making by a pension fund? As the focus of analysis of value-based ALM is economic value, the analytical framework of this approach will therefore differ from standard ALM. *Classical ALM* usually uses items like the expected value of core variables supplemented with one or more measures of the degree of riskiness of those variables. Classical ALM often makes use of techniques like Monte Carlo simulations to project these distributions and to optimize the strategy of the fund. This output remains useful because it provides insight in the distribution of future possible results. One gets information on the probability of underfunding, the probability of a high contribution rate or probability of a low indexation or no indexation at all, and so on. This will give some idea as to the sustainability of the pension deal in the long run.

Value-based ALM essentially uses the same output of scenario analysis as classical ALM, however the future outcomes are discounted back to the present with an appropriate risk adjusted discount rate. This is realized by discounting with either deflators, risk neutral valuation or pricing kernels (compare the contributions of Hibbert *et al.* (2006), and Nijman and Koijen (2006) *in this volume*).

---

[3] Major trends are IFRS (International Financial Reporting Standards) using fair value concepts and supervision in countries in Europe. In the Netherlands the government and supervisor are working on a fair value framework to be implemented January 1, 2007.

The shift from classical ALM to value-based ALM leads to at least two types of extra insights. The first new insight is the value the (financial) market currently attaches to future cash flows. ALM experts looked at averages, shortfalls etc., but disregarded information given by financial markets in the form of the present value of the future cash flows. Since the market is risk averse, one can learn that a deal with low average contributions can have a high present value for these contributions, especially if future contributions can be high in expensive states as often is the case in periods of low investment returns/funding ratios.[4] The opportunity the fund has to increase contributions in economic bad times will have a high present value for the fund. Active members are the ones bearing this risk.

Value-based ALM can calculate the present value of cash flows like contributions and indexation since these cash flows – in the approach we use by making these contingent on the funding ratio – are linked to cash flows of financial titles like equities and bonds. Even if these cash flows are not fixed – like in the situation of conditional indexation based on an indexation ladder (also see Section 10.6.4) – their present value can be calculated using the concept of replicating portfolios (also see Exley (2006) *in this volume*). A pension fund can thus value all options it is holding in the form of all kinds of contribution and/or indexation policies.

In this chapter, apart from giving information about the present value of future cash flows in the form of present value of contributions and benefits, we also use 'option surplus' and 'option deficit,' the present value of future surpluses and deficits. These in our opinion give far more relevant information about the possible future surpluses/deficits than the likelihood and the depth of a possible shortfall or surplus.

The second new insight is that one can look at the stakes of various parties joining the pension fund and that one can see the impact of changing the pension deal on various stakeholders. This will help to formulate a more sustainable pension deal and to avoid that one group, for instance the young members, have to pay up for any shortfall but do not get compensated in getting extra upside at the same time. The new pension deal can have (substantial) negative impact on the present value for certain stakeholders, in our experience this information is an important addition to classical ALM.

As to our knowledge, the paper of Chapman *et al.* (2001) is the first contribution in this field. They apply the approach to strategic decision

---

[4]Also see Kortleve (2003).

making within a company pension fund organising a defined benefit plan. They model the fund not as a self-contained entity but simultaneously with the sponsoring company. The analysis is focused primarily on transfers of value between the shareholders and the pension fund participants. Ponds (2003b) and Kortleve (2003, 2004) employ the value-based approach to analyse transfers of value between old, young and future members within a pension fund where risk have to be borne primarily by the plan members. One may speak of intergenerational risk sharing that typically can be found in industry wide pension plans (the Netherlands) and public sector pension funds (UK, US, Canada). This contribution primarily is aimed at clarifying the main differences between classical ALM and value-based ALM.

A pension fund is a zero-sum game in economic value terms. A change in the pension fund strategy (for example taking more or less investment risk) does not create economic value, however it may lead to transfers of value between stakeholders. Value-based ALM facilitates in clarifying who gains and who loses in economic value terms from a given pension fund strategy or from a change in the strategy.[5] A pension fund being a zero-sum game in value terms can be a positive-sum game in utility terms. The final section of this chapter discusses implications if one incorporates welfare aspects in the analysis.

10.3. Characteristics of the pension fund

The pension fund has the following features:

1. Pension plan: average-wage plan with indexed liabilities. The indexation may be conditional depending on the content of the Pension Deal. The yearly indexation is aimed to follow the price inflation.
2. Liabilities: the valuation of the indexed liabilities is based on discounting with the real interest rate.[6] The duration of the indexed liabilities is 21 years (at a real rate of 2%). 60% of the participants is pensioner

---

[5]Assuming stakeholders will not compensate these changes using financial markets. If markets are complete and frictionless markets and there are no transaction costs etc., stakeholders could for instance use derivatives to hedge and offset the impact of the changes.
[6]Almost all Dutch pension plans assume nominal liabilities in accounting for their funding ratio for the new solvency test.

or deferred. The remaining part of 40% comprises the (current and future) active members.

3. Funding ratio: the initial real funding ratio is 100%. The real funding ratio is defined as the ratio of the value of the assets and the value of the indexed liabilities.

4. Contribution rate: the base contribution rate has to meet the economic costs ('cost price') of new liabilities accruing during one year of service based on the relevant discount rate, i.e., the real rate. The funding method is formulated for a going-concern pension fund: the base contribution rate to be asked in the coming 40 years P_t^* is solved from the requirement of a balance between the present value of new accrued liabilities in the coming 40 years and the present value of contributions in the coming 40 years:

$$P_t^* = \frac{\text{PV new liabilities 40 years}}{\text{PV pensionable wages 40 years}}$$

Contributions are expressed as a percentage of the pensionable wage income. As the target indexation is linked to the price inflation, the terms in the above formula for the base contribution rate is calculated with the expected real rate. The length of the 40 year period reflects the length of one generation.

5. Asset mix: we consider just two variants in the asset mix: 100% nominal bonds and 100% equities. The duration of the bonds is 5.3 years.

6. Policy horizon: we assume a policy horizon of 15 years.[7] This means that we assume a plan horizon of 15 years. During these 15 years new benefits are being built, benefits will accrue with the indexation being granted, the fund realizes investment returns etc.

7. Risk-bearing:[8] employers (in this chapter) are no risk-bearing party. The involvement of employers with the funding is restricted to paying contributions from gross wage income. Hence, all the funding risks have to

---

[7] The 15-year period is the length of the recovery period that pension funds in the Netherlands will be given to accumulate the required solvency buffer in case of a solvency deficit.

[8] The spectrum of pension funds shows up a great variety in the nature of risk bearing because the stakeholders are free in making rules as to who should bear the risks in the funding process. However, one may distinguish two basic types. The first one may be found in company pension plans, where it is usually prescribed that the sponsoring firm is solely responsible for the funding position. The second basic form can be found in public sector pension funds and industry pension funds where the funding risks typically are borne by the members collectively.

be borne by current and future members of the pension plan.[9] In Section 10.6 we will discuss four different variants of risk-bearing by the plan members.

10.4. Framework of analysis

The balance sheet of a pension fund in economic value terms will look as the one displayed in Figure 10.1. The represented terms are the economic value expressions at $t = 0$ of the relevant variables at the end of the horizon at $t = T$.

The term ΔInd_T may be negative or positive reflecting either a cut in full indexation or additional indexation above full indexation. The term ΔP_T also may be negative or positive reflecting either a reduction or an extra charge to the cost price contributions. The term R_T is the economic value of

Figure 10.1. Balance sheet pension fund in economic value terms

A_0	L_0
P_T	nL_T
ΔP_T	ΔInd_T
	R_T

where
A_0 = value of assets at $t = 0$
L_0 = value of accrued liabilities (with full indexation) at $t = 0$
nL_T = economic value of new accruing liabilities during the period $t = 0$ to $t = T$ (with full indexation)
P_T = economic value of contributions during the period $t = 0$ to $t = T$ to fund the new accruing liabilities nL_T
ΔInd_T = economic value of additional indexation apart from full indexation during the period $t = 0$ to $t = T$
ΔP_T = economic value of additional contributions apart from full cost price contributions P_T during the period $t = 0$ to $t = T$
R_T = economic value of funding residue at the end of year T

---

[9]This type of risk bearing is typical for industry pension funds in the Netherlands. There are around 80 industry pension funds in the Netherlands, covering almost 70% of the workers and more than 70% of total assets of Dutch pension funds of around 480 billion Euro (end of 2004). Around 25% of the working force is participant in a corporate pension fund. The remaining 5% of the workers has a defined contribution plan (3%) or no plan at all (2%).

the residue at the end of year T, and it may be either positive or negative as well.

As by definition the economic value of the cost price contributions equals the value of the new liabilities to be built up during the horizon under consideration, i.e., $P_T = nL_T$, and as the initial balance sheet at $t = 0$ is identical to: $A_0 = L_0 + R_0$, we can rearrange terms in the balance sheet of Figure 10.1. to get the fundamental expression below reflecting the nature of a pension fund of being a zero-sum game in economic value terms:

$$-\Delta P_T + \Delta \text{Ind}_T + \Delta R_T = 0$$

where:
$$\Delta R_T = R_T - R_0$$

This expression also clarifies that a pension fund has three methods of risk management:

1. Intertemporal spreading of risk: a funding surplus or a funding deficit is shifted forward in time. There is no active risk management at all.
2. Contribution adjustments: a funding surplus or a deficit is absorbed by workers via receiving a contribution cut or an extra contribution charge respectively. Total contributions are equal to the cost price contributions plus – some part of – the pension fund residue.
3. Indexation adjustments: the funding risks can be taken up by adjusting the indexation rate so that total indexation is equal to the total aimed indexation plus – some part of – the pension fund residue.[10]

The risk-adjusted discounting provides the economic value of the residue (at $t = T$) of this distribution at $t = 0$, R_T. The term R_T can be split up in two parts: the economic value of the surplus minus the economic value of the deficit.

$$
\begin{aligned}
R_T = {}&\text{economic value surplus} &-/-&\quad \text{economic value deficit} \\
&\quad\text{at } t = T && \quad\quad \text{at } t = T \\
= {}&\text{option price at } t = 0 \text{ of} &-/-&\quad \text{option price at } t = 0 \text{ of} \\
&\quad\text{surplus at } t = T && \quad\quad \text{deficit at } t = T
\end{aligned}
$$

------

[10]A fourth method may be reduction of nominal liabilities. Technically this may be processed by allowing negative indexation. The latter is possible within deal 3 (see Section 10.6.3).

The risk-bearing stakeholders have a call on the future surpluses and these surpluses will be distributed amongst them according to the risk-allocation rules of the pension deal in operation. In case of deficits the risk-bearing stakeholders have to make up the funding shortfall. This may be interpreted as if these stakeholders have written a put with an exercise price for the residue of zero, i.e., the economic cost of reinsurance against deficits at $t = T$. One may interpret the economic value of a surplus or a deficit as option premiums. Hence, the economic value of the surplus may be seen as the option premium for a call on the surplus at the end of period T, whereas the economic value of the deficit may be interpreted as the option price for a written put with an exercise price for the residue of zero.

10.5. Economic environment

10.5.1. Assumptions

The model being used for the calculations in this chapter is a modern version of Timbuk1.[11,12] The model is calibrated to the market prices as of December 31, 2003.

The pension fund outlook with respect to the economic future is captured in the expectations and volatility of the core economic variables as displayed in Table 10.1. Note that it is assumed that the wage inflation is equal to the price inflation, so the real growth rate of wages is zero.

10.5.2. Deflators

In this chapter we use deflators to discount the cash flows to arrive at the correct present value of these cash flows. Either deflators, risk neutral valuation or pricing kernels can be used to discount all kinds of future cash flows, including benefits, contributions and asset returns.[13] To get the present value of a financial title, one should multiply the possible cash flows of that title

---

[11] One can download documentation from http://www.gemstudy.com/FairValueDownloads/Timbuk1.pdf.

[12] For description of these types of models, also see the contributions of Hibbert *et al.* (2006) and Nijman and Koijen (2006) *in this volume.*

[13] See contributions of Hibbert *et al.* (2006) for concept of various approaches and how these approaches are linked to one another.

Table 10.1. Economic outlook

Economic variables	Expected outcome[1]	Standard deviation
Inflation[2]	3.2	1.5
Nominal rate of interest	5.6	1.6
Nominal bonds[3]	5.4	4.7
Real rate of interest[4]	2.0	0.5
Equities	10.8	26.3

[1]Geometric returns.

[2]It is assumed price inflation and wage inflation are the same, i.e., there is no real wage growth.

[3]Duration nominal bonds is 5.3 years, being the duration in the market.

[4]10 year zero rate.

by the corresponding deflators:

$$PV = \Sigma_i CF_i \times p_i \times D_i$$

Where

PV = present value

CF_i = cash flow in state i (assuming 1000 simulations, this can be any of the simulations)

p_i = probability of state i (e.g. 1 out of 1000)

D_i = deflator for state i

Deflators will correct for the equity risk premium relative to risk free assets. In other words, even though equities do show a higher expect return and therefore generate higher cash flows on average than bonds, the present value of 100 Euros in equities is (of course) the same as the present value of 100 Euros in bonds. High cash flows from equities will most of the time be multiplied by low deflators, whereas low cash flows will be multiplied by high deflators, as one can also see from Figure 10.2. The correlation between equity returns and deflators is negative, meaning that on average high equity returns will be multiplied by low deflators and vice versa. So, very poor equity returns of −50% can have a deflator of 3 or even more, whereas very attractive equity returns of +100% have deflators of 0.5 or below. For equities the present value of a cash flow of 100 in poor times can be 10 times as high as in prosperous times. As one can see from the figure, there is hardly any correlation between bond returns and deflators, which means that high bond returns are – on average – not compensated by low deflators and vice versa.

Figure 10.2. Equity and bond returns versus deflators

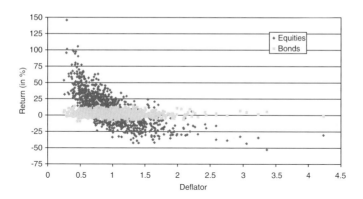

10.6. Variants in funding strategy and risk bearing

We will discuss four distinctive pension deals. This enables us to show the impact of alternative pension deals on the value of the stakes of the stakeholders. These deals differ as to the contribution policy, the indexation policy, the asset mix and risk allocation.

With the term 'pension deal' we mean the contract between the pension fund and the stakeholders that sets out the nature of the pension promise (final pay or average wage, the nature of the indexation policy), the funding of this promise and how the risks in the funding process are allocated (implicit or explicit) amongst the stakeholders. An explicit pension deal has clear rules prescribing who has to pay, when and to what extent in a deficit situation. These rules also set down who will benefit, when, and to what extent in a surplus situation. Below we discuss four examples of explicit deals. The deals investigated are:

Variants in funding strategy and risk bearing

Pension deal	Risk management	Indexation policy	Contribution policy
1. No active risk management	None	Full	Fixed
2. Pure defined benefit	Steering using contributions	Full	Contingent on funding ratio

continued

Variants in funding strategy and risk bearing—Cont'd

Pension deal	Risk management	Indexation policy	Contribution policy
3. Collective defined contribution	Steering using indexation	Indexation accrued rights contingent on funding ratio	Fixed
4. Policy ladder	Using both indexation and contribution to steer	Indexation accrued rights contingent on funding ratio with minimum and maximum	Contingent on funding ratio with minimum and maximum

10.6.1. Deal 1: No active risk management (Spreading risk over time/risk spreading between generations)

Pension deal 1 is characterized by no active risk management at all. There is no aim to correct the course of the funding ratio over time by making use of either the indexation instrument or the contribution policy. Each year the contribution rate is set equal to the cost price to fund new accrued liabilities and every year the indexation follows the actual inflation (see Figure 10.3) This deal has a maximum appeal on spreading risk over time, or in other words on intergenerational risk-sharing. Actually, the pension fund relies on an infinite sequence of overlapping age-cohorts. Table 10.2 reflects the core results in terms of expected values and riskiness of the variables for a mix of 100% bonds and a mix of 100% equities, respectively. This is the usual classical ALM output.

Figure 10.3.   Pension deal 1: No active risk management

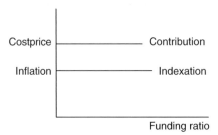

Table 10.2. Classic ALM results deal 1

	MIX = 100% Bonds 2005–2019	MIX = 100% Equities 2005–2019
Funding ratio		
average	99.0	180.9
risk (st dev)	2.7	132.8
st dev D FR	1.0	45.0
prob underfunding	70.4	29.7
Contributions		
average	21.4	21.4
risk	1.5	1.5
Relative pension result	100%	100%
Indexation		
none	0%	0%
partial	0%	0%
full	100%	100%
catch up	0%	0%

As can be read from Table 10.2, the cost price contribution rate is slightly higher than 21% of pensionable wages. Indexation is always linked to the actual inflation, so the cumulative indexation has a full 100% match with the target indexation. The mix consisting of 100% nominal bond delivers on average a real rate of return of 2% as anticipated in setting the contribution rate. Therefore the funding ratio on average remains stable over time. The volatility in the funding ratio is quite low primarily because of the low risk in the real rate and because of the high correlation between the real rate and the nominal rate. The 100% bonds mix nevertheless will imply some mismatch risk, firstly because the pay-off structure of nominal bonds differs from the growth rate of indexed liabilities as there is no perfect correlation between nominal rate and real rate, and secondly because the duration of the liabilities is much higher than the duration of the bond mix.

The 100% equity mix gives prospect to a higher expected real return compared with the real rate, so the expected funding ratio will increase over time. This investment strategy implies a much higher risk profile for the stakeholders than the investment strategy with 100% bonds. This can be checked with Table 10.2 by looking at the risk measures of the funding ratio that quantify the spreading in the funding ratio, i.e., the standard deviation of the funding ratio itself (almost 133% for equities and just 3% for bonds) and of the change in the funding ratio in one year (45% for equities and just 1% for bonds).

Figures 10.4 and 10.5 show the development of the funding ratio for the two investment strategies.[14] The risky 100% equity strategy leads on average to an increase in the funding ratio, and so to an increasing funding surplus. The funding ratio of the low risky 100% bond strategy remains stable over time.

Table 10.3 shows the results of value-based ALM. The balance sheets reflect economic values. Note that the economic value of the funding residue of both strategies is the same! This is to be explained by the high economic value attached to underfunding and the low economic value of overfunding.

Figure 10.4. *Funding ratio in deal 1 with 100% bonds*

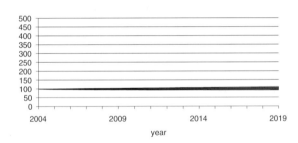

Figure 10.5. *Funding ratio in deal 1 with 100% equities*

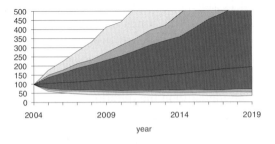

---

[14]The graphs show the following percentiles of the probability distribution of the funding ratio: 1, 5, 10, 90, 95, 99 and the median.

Table 10.3. Value-based ALM results deal 1

100% Bonds			
Assets (A_0)	**100**	Accrued liabilities (L_0)	**100**
Contributions (P_T)	**90**	New liabilities (nL_T)	**90**
Additional contributions	**0**	Additional indexation	**0**
		Change residue (ΔR_T)	**0**
		Option surplus	**4**
		Option deficit	**−4**

100% Equities			
Assets (A_0)	**100**	Accrued liabilities (L_0)	**100**
Contributions (P_T)	**90**	New liabilities (nL_T)	**90**
Additional contributions	**0**	Additional indexation	**0**
		Change residue (ΔR_T)	**0**
		Option surplus	**50**
		Option deficit	**−49**

The 100% equity strategy may lead to a lower probability of underfunding, however when it occurs, underfunding may be sizeable and it most likely will happen in expensive states when stakeholders will not be able and willing to make up for shortfalls. It is very expensive to hedge a situation of underfunding. The deflator method attaches a high present value to outcomes in economic bad times. Deep underfunding typically will occur in bad times. The 100% bond strategy will have less underfunding in bad times, less both in terms of frequency and depth.

Our conclusion is that the assumed attractiveness of equities, as can be read from the classical Table 10.2, is not so attractive when viewed from the perspective of fair value. Equities do not add economic value; they increase the present value of future surpluses as well as the present value of future deficits![15] Fair value shows that taking risk does not increase the present value.

---

[15]The higher the volatility, the higher the value of an option price.

10.6.2. Deal 2: Pure defined benefit

The characteristics of deal 2 are in line with a pure defined benefit scheme: indexation is always given according to the promise and the contribution rate is adjusted yearly in order to absorb the risk in the pension fund. The target funding ratio is defined as the 100% funding ratio, this is the situation where the assets A_t are equal to the value of the indexed liabilities L_t, i.e., $A_t/L_t = 100\%$. The contribution rate will be equal to the cost price when the funding ratio is 100%. Any deviation between the actual and the target funding ratio will lead to an adjustment in the contribution rate. There is a cut in case of overfunding, whereas a charge is asked in case of underfunding. Full adjustment of the funding ratio back to the target level in one year will lead to extreme adjustments in the contribution. Therefore the fund aims to reach the full funding situation after 40 years. So the restoration of any deviation of the actual funding ratio from its target level is smoothed out over a period of 40 years. Hence, the additional contribution rate apart from the base rate, P_t^{add}, is calculated as follows (also see Figure 10.6):

$$P_t^{\text{add}} = \frac{\text{Liabilities} - \text{Assets}}{\text{PV pensionable wages 40 years}}$$

The total contribution rate is equal to the sum of cost price contribution rate plus the additional contribution rate:

$$\text{Total Contribution Rate} = P_t^* + P_t^{\text{add}}$$

Figure 10.6.   Deal 2: Pure defined benefit

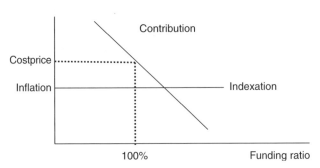

Table 10.4. Classic ALM results deal 2

	MIX = 100% Bonds 2005–2019	MIX = 100% Equities 2005–2019
Funding ratio		
average	**99**	**172.7**
risk (st dev)	**2.5**	**118.5**
st dev D FR	**1**	**42.9**
prob underfunding	**68.7**	**29.6**
Contributions		
average	**21.5**	**13.3**
risk	**1.6**	**13.5**
Relative pension result	**100%**	**100%**
Indexation		
none	**0%**	**0%**
partial	**0%**	**0%**
full	**100%**	**100%**
catch up	**0%**	**0%**

The classical ALM results are quite familiar (Table 10.4). The contribution rate in the equity strategy displays on average a downward trend (Figure 10.7). The on average high excess return in this strategy is translated in cuts in the contribution rate. The average contribution rate drops from 21.4% to only 13.3%, though the latter has more dispersion and can be higher than 30% in some more extreme cases. The bond strategy delivers

Figure 10.7. Contribution rate in deal 2 with 100% bonds

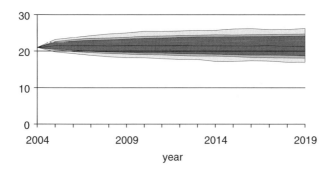

Figure 10.8.   Contribution rate in deal 2 with 100% equities

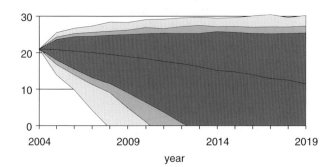

year

no excess return, so the contribution rate in this strategy equals the cost price contribution rate, which fluctuates depending on the future real rate (Figures 10.7 and 10.8).

When we compare the classical results of deal 2 with deal 1, we note that the variability in the funding ratio has declined somewhat due to the shifting of part of the mismatch risk towards the contribution rate and thus to (future) active members. This may be seen from the value-based results as well (Table 10.5).

The decline in variability of the residue is also reflected in the option values of a surplus or deficit. These values have decreased due to the reduction in the dispersion of the funding ratio. Furthermore, note that the value of additional contributions (cuts as well as charges) is positive, i.e., active workers will pay a higher contribution on balance in economic value terms compared with deal 1. This is easily explained if one recognizes that contribution charges typically will be asked in economic bad times and so these charges may have a high economic value, whereas contribution cuts are given usually in good times and so will have a low economic value. The counterpart is that the economic value of the residue increases. The dispersion in the residue decreases in deal 2 compared with deal 1, and the economic value of the decrease in probability and size of underfunding is – in economic value terms – more valuable than the decrease in probability and size of overfunding.

10.6.3. Deal 3: Collective defined contribution

Deal 3 may be seen as the counterpart of deal 2. The contribution rate is set equal to the base contribution rate and the indexation rate is used as the

Table 10.5. *Value-based ALM results deal 2*

100% Bonds			
Assets (A_0)	100	Accrued liabilities (L_0)	100
Contributions (P_T)	90	New liabilities (nL_T)	90
Additional contributions	2	Additional indexation	0
		Change residue (ΔR_T)	1
		Option surplus	4	
		Option deficit	−4	
100% Equities			
Assets (A_0)	100	Accrued liabilities (L_0)	100
Contributions (P_T)	90	New liabilities (nL_T)	90
Additional contributions	2	Additional indexation	0
		Change residue (ΔR_T)	1
		Option surplus	22	
		Option deficit	−21	

instrument to control risk. The indexation rate will be equal to the actual price inflation when the funding ratio is equal to its target level of 100%. Any deviation between the actual funding ratio and the target funding ratio will lead to an adjustment in the indexation rate. The additional indexation is calculated as the ratio of the residue to the present value of the projected liabilities[16] (compare Figure 10.9):

$$\Delta \text{Ind}_t = \frac{\text{Assets} - \text{Liabilities}}{\text{PV projected Liabilities}}$$

Note that to the analogy with deal 2, risk bearing is spread out over current and future members as the restoration of any deviation of the actual

---

[16]The present value of the projected liabilities is the sum of the present value of the currently accrued liabilities plus the present value of the new liabilities to be accruing in the coming 15 years.

funding ratio from its target is smoothed out over time, over already accrued
and newly accruing liabilities.

   This deal implies that any deviation of the funding ratio of its target will
lead to a deviation between the aimed indexation and the actual indexation.
The 100% equity mix on average has a high return and this high return will
be given away in additional indexation. In 55% of the cases, the funding
ratio is above 100% and so the pension fund pays out more than just full
indexation (Figure 10.10). The relative pension result indexation reaches an
average value of 205%! The relative pension result is defined as the ratio of
the actual pension result to the target pension result. However, the dispersion
is also very high as can be seen from Figure 10.11.

   When we take notice of the economic value consequences of this deal,
then another picture arises. In 38% of the cases during the period under
consideration, assets fall below the value of nominal liabilities so then there

Figure 10.9.   Deal 3: Collective defined contribution

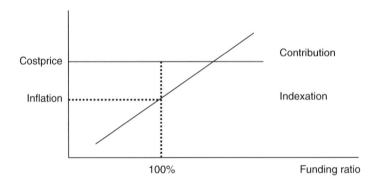

Figure 10.10.   Relative pension result in deal 3 with 100% bonds

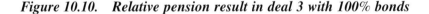
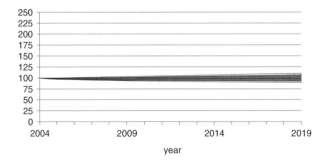

is negative indexation, i.e., a cut in the accrued liabilities. In 7% of the cases, the value of the assets falls between the value of the nominal liabilities and the value of the real liabilities and so there is room for partial indexation. Indexation cuts and negative indexation will occur in particular during bad times. The economic value of these cuts therefore will be so high that they by far outweigh the economic value of the additional indexation being given in 55% of the cases.

This deal shows up a dramatic difference between classical and value-based ALM (see Tables 10.6 and 10.7). Value-based ALM shows once again

Figure 10.11. *Relative pension result in deal 3 with 100% equities*

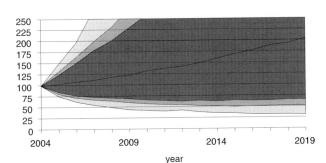

year

Table 10.6. *Classic ALM results deal 3*

	MIX = 100% Bonds 2005–2019	MIX = 100% Equities 2005–2019
Funding ratio		
average	100	109
risk (st dev)	1.1	26.9
st dev D FR	1.3	33.1
prob underfunding	49.2	41.0
Contributions		
average	21.4	21.4
risk	1.5	1.5
Relative pension result	100%	205%
Indexation		
negative	10%	38%
less than full	43%	7%
more than full	47%	55%

Table 10.7. Value-based ALM results deal 3

		100% Bonds		
Assets (A_0)	**100**	Accrued liabilities (L_0)		**100**
Contributions (P_T)	**90**	New liabilities (nL_T)		**90**
Additional contributions	**0**	Additional indexation		**−2**
		Change residue (ΔR_T)		**4**
		Option surplus	**4**	
		Option deficit	**−1**	
		100% Equities		
Assets (A_0)	**100**	Accrued liabilities (L_0)		**100**
Contributions (P_T)	**90**	New liabilities (nL_T)		**90**
Additional contributions	**0**	Additional indexation		**−2**
		Change residue (ΔR_T)		**4**
		Option surplus	**18**	
		Option deficit	**−14**	

that the extra indexation comes in good times, so the present value of these 55% of the scenarios does not outweigh the other 45%; the present value is the same for the portfolio of 100% bonds and of 100% equities.

10.6.4. Deal 4: Policy ladder

A number of Dutch pension funds recently has introduced a so-called policy ladder, in Dutch '*Beleidsstaffel*' (Ponds, 2003a). We may interpret the ladder as a combination of components of the two preceding deals. The basic idea of the ladder is quite simple. We explain the basic idea with the help of Figure 10.12. Two points are of crucial importance, the upper bound and the lower bound. It is assumed in this chapter that the upper bound is the situation where the real funding ratio is 100%, this is when the assets exactly match the value of the indexed liabilities. The lower bound is the situation where the nominal funding ratio is 100%, i.e., the value of the assets is the same as the value of the nominal liabilities (thus no indexation). The difference between

Figure 10.12.   Deal 4: Policy ladder

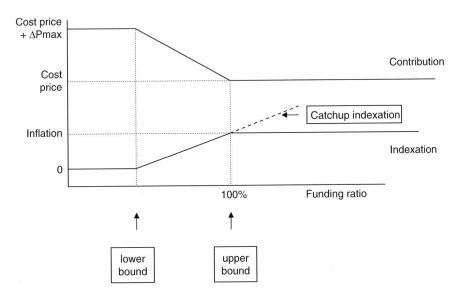

the upper bound and lower bound is the necessary indexation reserve needed to pay for the future indexation of the accrued liabilities. This indexation reserve can also be expressed as the difference between the value of indexed liabilities (based on the real yield curve) and the value of nominal liabilities (with valuation based on the nominal yield curve).

The contribution rate and the indexation are set along the vertical axis.

Indexation policy: The magnitude of the indexation is related proportionally to the size of the available indexation reserve, this is the difference between assets and nominal liabilities. There is room for full indexation, if and when the value of the assets equals the value of fully indexed liabilities. In this case, the actual indexation reserve matches the required indexation reserve. The indexation rate will be zero when the assets are equal to or even below the present value of the nominal liabilities. The indexation reserve then is actually zero or even negative. Between these points there will be an indexation cut where the size of the cut is related to the actual deficit in indexation reserve. Whenever the value of the assets exceeds the value of indexed liabilities, there is room to provide extra indexation until there is a full catching-up of previously missed indexation.

Figure 10.13. Contribution rate in deal 4 with 100% bonds

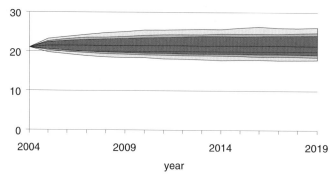

Figure 10.14. Contribution rate in deal 4 with 100% equities

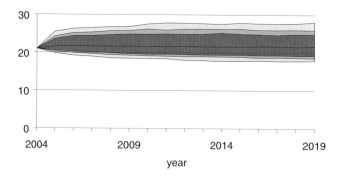

Contribution rate: The contribution rate is set equal to the cost price of
the new accrued liabilities of one year of service when the funding
ratio is equal to or is higher than 100%.[17] A contribution charge is
levied when assets fall short of the indexed liabilities. To the analogy
with the indexation cut, the charge will increase when the deficit is
increasing. The maximum charge is determined by the annual funding
costs in order to build up the required indexation reserve within 40 years
(Figures 10.13 and 10.14).

From the classical ALM results we make up that the 100% bonds strategy on average yields a funding ratio of around 100% (Table 10.8). The
contribution rate is on average around the cost price level. The median

---

[17]The pension fund could also decide to cut the contribution below cost price, when the plan is
overfunded (i.e., funding ratio is higher than 100%).

Table 10.8. Classic ALM results deal 4

	MIX = 100% Bonds 2005–2019	MIX = 100% Equities 2005–2019
Funding ratio		
average	99.2	182.7
risk (st dev)	2.5	131.8
st dev D FR	1	45.2
prob underfunding	68.4	28.5
Contributions		
average	21.5	21.9
risk	1.6	2
Relative pension result	100%	100%
Indexation		
none	0%	3%
partial	32%	22%
full	49%	47%
catch up	19%	28%

Figure 10.15. Relative pension result in deal 4 with 100% bonds

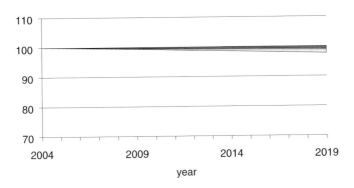

cumulative indexation equals 100%, being the result of both indexation cuts and catch-up indexation. The 100% equity mix will lead on average to an ever increasing funding ratio as the expected high equity return cannot be translated in cuts in the contribution rate as in deal 2 or in additional indexation as in deal 3. The average funding ratio is increasingly much higher than 100%.

The value-based ALM results make clear that the 100% equity strategy does not necessarily imply better results in economic value terms. After adjusting the future results for the high risk involvement it becomes clear that the costs of additional contributions and indexation cuts are very high and take away the general believed advantages of risk-taking. The high equity returns turn up in economic times with low deflators and therefore have limited present value, at least lower than their nominal cash flows do imply. The low equity returns coincide with high deflators as well as with higher contributions and lower indexation. So when equities perform poor, the members are hurt by extra payments to the fund and lower pensions out of the fund (Figure 10.15).

Further note that with 100% equities the current stakeholders are losing economic value (compare 100% equities with 100% bonds in Table 10.9). There is an increase of +20 in the value of the future residue in comparison with deal 1. This increase is primarily due to indexation cuts during bad periods for equity investments (note the additional indexation is −16, also

Table 10.9.   Value-based ALM results deal 4

100% Bonds				
Assets (A_0)	100	Accrued liabilities (L_0)		100
Contributions (P_T)	90	New liabilities (nL_T)		90
Additional contributions	1	Additional indexation		0
		Change residue (ΔR_T)		2
		Option surplus	4	
		Option deficit	−2	
100% Equities				
Assets (A_0)	100	Accrued liabilities (L_0)		100
Contributions (P_T)	90	New liabilities (nL_T)		90
Additional contributions	6	Additional indexation		−16
		Change residue (ΔR_T)		20
		Option surplus	50	
		Option deficit	−31	

Figure 10.16. **Relative pension result in deal 4 with 100% equities**

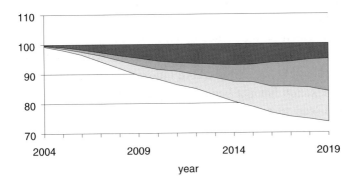

Figure 10.17. **Change in economic value per age cohort**

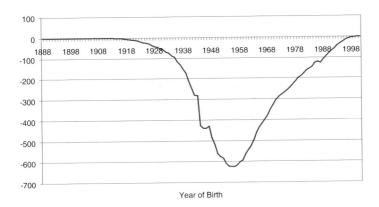

see Figure 10.16) and also because of extra contributions during these bad periods (note additional contribution is +6, also see Figure 10.14).

Figure 10.17 clarifies who is paying for this increase in the funding residue. We have displayed the change in economic value per age cohorts when the pension fund steps over from deal 2 (or deal 1 or deal 3) to deal 4. We see that all cohorts lose economic value by this change. The fund collectively benefits, since the present value of the residue increases relative to the previous deals. Future generations will be more willing to join this deal since the present value for them more likely will be positive. Why do current members lose on average? Active workers have to pay additional contributions when the funding ratio falls below the upper bound, however there are no contribution cuts when the funding ratio is higher than the upper bound. So workers pay on balance more contributions in deal 4 compared to deal 2. There are indexation cuts when the funding ratio falls short of the upper bound. Catch-up indexation is given when the funding ratio is recovered above the upper bound. On balance, cohorts will lose economic value because there will be scenarios where indexation cuts have been passed but catch-up indexation has not been given yet or only partially. Extending the horizon will lead to a decrease in the shortage. The relative reduction in shortage for a specific cohort will be larger the younger a cohort is.

10.7. From value to welfare

An important result of value-based ALM is that it shows that a pension fund is a zero-sum game in economic value terms. This insight may suggest that any pension fund policy only implies transfers of value amongst the stakeholders which do not have any role (cf. Exley, 2004). However this conclusion neglects the welfare aspects of pension funds. Indeed pension funds are potentially welfare-enhancing because pension funds aim to offer retirement income products which are not available in the market.[18] Although the offered insurance may differ amongst the various pension funds, the aim of the different pension deals is to enable the participant to go on with the standard of living before retirement after one is retired. This kind of 'insurance' offers protection against the risk that the purchasing power of pension savings is eroded by inflation and also against the risk that pension savings do not hold pace with the real growth of the economy, i.e., the general standard of living. From the literature, it is well-known that these types of insurance can be organized by intergenerational risk-sharing. Just because the market fails to organize this kind of risk-sharing, pension funds are potentially welfare-enhancing (Gordon and Varian, 1988; Shiller, 1999; Ponds, 2003b). Cui *et al.* (2005) developed a framework wherein pension funds can be evaluated in economic value terms as well as in utility terms. The utility analysis clarifies the welfare aspects of pension funds. They show first that in utility terms a pension fund as a risk-sharing arrangement is more useful than an

---

[18]Even if markets are complete and stakeholders do have full insight in and understanding of their stakes (i.e., contributions, benefits and indexation), cutting costs, sharing risks and other arguments still seem to favour collective pensions over individual pensions.

individual pension saving program without risk-sharing opportunities (individual defined contribution plan), and secondly that pension deals being performed by pension funds are ranked higher in utility terms the more they contribute to safe and smoothed consumption patterns over the life-cycle of the involved participants. Indeed a pension fund always is a zero-sum game in value terms, however it is potentially a positive-sum game in welfare terms.

References

Ambachtsheer, K.A. (2006), Building Better Pension Plans on a 'Fair Value' Foundation, *this volume*.

Chapman, R.J., T.J. Gordon and C.A. Speed (2001), "Pensions, funding and risk", *British Actuarial Journal*, Vol. 74, pp. 605–663.

Cui, J., F. Jong de and E.H.M. Ponds (2005), Intergenerational Transfers within Funded Pension Schemes, working paper, Netspar, University of Tilburg.

Exley, J. (2004), Stakeholders Interests Alignment/Agency Issues, paper presented at the International Centre for Pension Management Colloquium October 5–6 2004, University of Toronto.

Exley, J. (2006), The Fair Value Principle, *this volume*.

Gordon, R.H. and H.R. Varian (1988), "Intergenerational risk-sharing", *Journal of Public Economics*, Vol. 14, pp. 1–29.

Hibbert, J., S. Morrison and C. Turnbull (2006), Techniques for Market-consistent Valuation of Contingent Claims, *this volume*.

Kortleve, C.E. (2003), "De meerwaarde van beleidsopties", *Economisch-Statistische Berichten*, 12 December 2003, pp. 588–590 (English translation available).

Kortleve, C.E. (2004), "De marktwaarde van beleggingsopties", *VBA Journaal*, No. 2, summer 2004, pp. 32–36.

Nijman, T. and R. Koijen (2006), Valuation and Risk Management of Inflation-sensitive Pension Rights, *this volume*.

Ponds, E.H.M. (2003a), "Fair pensioen voor jong en oud", *Economisch-Statistische Berichten*, 24 January 2003, pp. 28–31.

Ponds, E.H.M. (2003b), "Pension funds and value-based generational accounting", *Journal of Pension Economics and Finance*, Vol. 2, No. 3, pp. 295–325.

Shiller, R.J. (1999), "Social security and institutions for intergenerational, intragenerational and international risk sharing", *Carnegie-Rochester Conference Series on Public Policy*, Vol. 50, pp. 165–204.